SHAKESPEARE'S
GUIDE TO LIVING THE GOOD LIFE

SHAKESPEARE'S
GUIDE TO LIVING THE GOOD LIFE

*Life Lessons for
Comedy, Tragedy,
and Everything
in Between*

KIM BRADLEY

Hierophantpublishing

Copyright © 2025 by Kim Bradley

All rights reserved, including the right to reproduce this work in any form whatsoever, without permission in writing from the publisher, except for brief passages in connection with a review.

Quotes from Shakespeare's works are made with reference to the Folger Shakespeare Library's editions.

Cover design by Laura Beers
Cover art by Shutterstock
Print book interior design by Frame25 Productions

Hierophant Publishing
San Antonio, TX
www.hierophantpublishing.com

If you are unable to order this book from your local bookseller, you may order directly from the publisher.

Library of Congress Control Number: 2024951741
ISBN: 978-1-950253-57-9

For Kate and Jane

When e'er I think on you, my darling twins,
All losses are restored and sorrows end.

Contents

Introduction   1

1. Hospitality
The Comedy of Errors   9

2. Imagination
A Midsummer Night's Dream   27

3. Compassion
The Merchant of Venice   45

4. Persistence
All's Well That Ends Well   61

5. Communication
Much Ado About Nothing   77

6. Communing with Nature
As You Like It   93

7. Thinking for Yourself
Julius Caesar   111

8. Being of Service
Twelfth Night   125

9. Friendship
The Winter's Tale   143

10. Forgiveness
The Tempest   159

Epilogue: You Are Divine
Sonnet 18   175

Acknowledgments   179

Notes   181

About the Author   187

Introduction

I know a bank where the wild thyme blows, where oxlips and the nodding violet grows, quite over-canopied with luscious woodbine, with sweet musk-roses and with eglantine...
—*A Midsummer Night's Dream*, act 1, scene 1

Close your eyes and imagine yourself in this space, surrounded by colorful flowers, murmuring water, and gentle thyme-scented tendrils of air. An oasis, a locus of refuge and quiet serenity, far away from the rattle and hum of daily life. Breathe deeply as you imagine yourself swaddled in the tranquility of this natural sanctuary. Read the quote again, drinking in the words as you inhale and exhale slowly.

You have just experienced the gift of William Shakespeare. A mere twenty-seven words of his iambic pentameter have the power to transport us to an enchanting summer afternoon. This is one of the many reasons why Shakespeare's works continue to be explored and adored.

The Bard of Avon, aka William Shakespeare, offers a multitude of treasures like these lines from *A Midsummer Night's Dream*. With 154 sonnets and over 30 of the most famous plays in recorded history in his oeuvre, Shakespeare is a treasure trove of creativity, inspiration, and freehearted observations about relationships. And not just romantic relationships (although he had much to say about Cupid's domain), but also our relationships with nature, commerce, systems of governance, music, our bodies, the cosmos, and God.

I wrote this book because Shakespeare's treasures are as relevant to us today as they were in the tumultuous, plague-ridden time during which Shakespeare lived. Do you sometimes feel overwhelmed, lost, or isolated? Do you struggle to find purpose and meaning in your life during the rough days we all encounter? Shakespeare gets you. Even better, he has some great insights that can guide us through those feelings and into the good life.

I had a crush on William Shakespeare "the writer" before I had any idea what he had written, thanks to a weekly magazine insert that my grandmother read in the Sunday paper. The insert, called "The Parade," featured a list of famous birthdays for the week, and I was five years old when my grandmother exclaimed, "You and William Shakespeare share a birthday!" I had been reading since the age of three, and I loved fairy tales, libraries, poems, pencils, the smell of paper, and storytelling more than anything in the world. Sharing a natal aspect with a famous writer seemed like a sign that we were meant to have a lifelong affair (which we have).

The more I learned about William Shakespeare, the more enthralled I became with his story. He was a country boy, raised in a small village along the outer fringes of the Forest of Arden, a place much like the farming community turned suburb where I was raised. Although Oxford and Cambridge had been educating the elite members of British society since 1096 and 1209, respectively, Shakespeare attended neither of them. He became one of the most revered playwrights of Western civilization despite (or maybe because of?) his lack of formal schooling. His success emerged from his ability to creatively convey his personal observations about the world, not from following the conventional rhetoric of the time. Honesty, originality, and playfulness are his hallmarks, and likely the very reasons why his art has endured.

My love affair with Shakespeare has lasted throughout my life, and he never ceases to surprise and delight. How could the person who wrote snarky gems such as "the first thing we do, let's kill all the lawyers" (*Henry VI*) and "thine face is not worth sunburning" (*Henry V*) also have written passionate poetry like this: "doubt thou the stars are fire, doubt that the sun doth move, doubt truth to be a liar, but never doubt I love" (*Hamlet*)?

Why do we still say today that mediocre things are "so-so" (*As You Like It*)? Why is overcoming the fear of connecting with others called "breaking the ice" (*The Taming of the Shrew*)? Why is no cap described as the "naked truth" (*Love's*

Introduction   3

Labour's Lost)? Why do we say that we live in a "brave new world" (*The Tempest*)?

Why, you ask? Because Shakespeare allowed himself to feel all the feels, and then used his singular talents to express his point of view through a medium that he loved. That's why his words are so relevant today. "So-so" describes the monotonous numbness that many of us feel in our lives. "Breaking the ice" takes enormous strength and is often a difficult process, but once it happens, we get to experience the flow. Telling the "naked truth" by sharing our authentic selves with others is the ultimate form of vulnerability. Living in a "brave new world" acknowledges that it takes courage to embrace change, especially on a collective level.

Shakespeare's deep dive into the human condition and his passion for sharing his insights with the world have enriched my life in so many practical ways. That's why I want to share his guide to living the good life with you. The best part is that you don't have to have an encyclopedic knowledge of Shakespeare's works to get the most out of this book. England's national poet is much more accessible than we've been led to believe; he's got something for everyone.

Have you been in love? Shakespeare's got loads to say about that: "When Love speaks, the voice of all the gods make heaven drowsy with the harmony" (*Love's Labour's Lost*); and "My bounty is as boundless as the sea, my love as deep. The more I give to thee, the more I have, for both are infinite" (*Romeo and Juliet*).

Or perhaps you, like Hamlet, have suffered the "pangs of despised love" and want nothing to do with romance right now. Shakespeare has even more to say about that, including some stinging insults: "I had rather hear my dog bark at a crow than a man swear he loves me" (*Much Ado About Nothing*); and "He's a most notable coward, an infinite and endless liar, an hourly promise-breaker, the owner of no one good quality" (*All's Well That Ends Well*).

Do you feel restored by communing with nature? Shakespeare was a nature lover as well: "We were as twinned lambs that did frisk i'th'sun" (*The Winter's Tale*); and "Come unto these yellow sands and then take hands, curtsied when you have and kissed the wild waves whist" (*The Tempest*).

Are you intrigued by politics or business? So was Shakespeare, who obviously felt some kind of way about them: "The abuse of greatness is when it disjoins remorse from power" (*Julius Caesar*); and "Though inclination be as sharp as will, my stronger guilt defeats my strong intent and, like a man to double business bound, I stand in pause where I shall first begin, and both neglect" (*Hamlet*).

Do you have a bawdy sense of humor? Shakespeare rarely resisted the temptation to add a bit of toilet or sexual humor to his plays. Here's one from *Venus and Adonis*: "Graze on my lips, and if those hills be dry, stray lower, where the pleasant

Introduction

fountains lie." And here's perhaps the original fart joke: "A man may break a word with you sir, and words are but wind. Ay, and break it in your face, so he break it not behind" (*The Comedy of Errors*).

Are you interested in the movement of the moon and stars? Shakespeare was too: "The sun's a thief, and with his great attraction robs the vast sea; the moon's an arrant thief, and her pale fire she snatches from the sun" (*Timon of Athens*).

You get the gist. Shakespeare lived in a time much like our own—overrun with political turmoil, divisiveness, war, extreme weather, recurrent plagues, the fouling of natural resources, and discrimination against people who were different. Yet amid the backdrop of those challenges, Shakespeare showed us what was important by doing what he loved. The performances of his works with his best friends and acting colleagues, the Lord Chamberlain's Men, brought a bit of joy to the lives of his neighbors, even if it was only for a few hours during a matinee or evening performance at the Globe Theatre, the Curtain, or Blackfriars indoor playhouse.

Shakespeare offers us, his world-weary audience, the same respite and inspiration today. His humor, depth of emotion, keen political analysis, innovative use of words and phrases, appreciation for the natural world, and understanding of human behavior have drawn us a map to the good life. Yes, there is sickness, death, conflict, and division in today's world. But there are also sunrises, starry skies, families, friendships, laughter, and love. Shakespeare invites us to enjoy the latter while acknowledging the former and shows how balancing an appreciation for both is key to living the good life.

Each chapter of this book features a play by William Shakespeare, summarized briefly so you'll always know the main story; a theme related to the good life that threads its way through the play; some history and context to bring the Elizabethan era to life; the science of well-being as it relates to each play's theme; and several enactments so you can apply some of Shakespeare's hard-won insights to the theater of your own life.

Grab your favorite beverage, get cozy, and immerse yourself in the Bard of Avon's enchanting form of entertainment, which is not only delightful in its artistry, but offers a gold mine of practical advice to enhance our lives. Hey nonny nonny and huzzah!

Chapter One

Hospitality

The Comedy of Errors

Duke Egeon and his wife Emilia are parents of identical twin boys, both named Antipholus. (It is called *The Comedy of Errors*, after all.) As luck would have it, on the very same day their twins are born, another set of identical twin boys, both named Dromio, are born to a woman who cannot care for them. Egeon and Emilia agree to take in the Dromios and raise them as their sons' attendants. The young family is shipwrecked in a storm while traveling on the duke's business, and the crew absconds with the lifeboat, leaving the brood of six to a watery grave.

Emilia ties the older Antipholus and older Dromio to one side of the listing ship's mast, and the younger Antipholus and Dromio are lashed to the other side, in hopes that the floating hunk of timber will keep them safe. Emilia stays with the older twins and Egeon remains on the opposite side with the younger twins. The mast collides with a huge rock, splitting the log in two and separating the boys and the parents. Egeon is rescued by a passing ship, along with the younger Antipholus and Dromio, but his wife and the older Antipholus and Dromio are picked up by a different ship and taken away, the family torn apart forever.

Many years pass, and when the younger Antipholus turns eighteen, he sets out with his sidekick Dromio to find their lost twin brothers. When they fail to return, Egeon travels by ship to look for them.

The play begins with Egeon under arrest in Ephesus as a pawn in a political battle between the Greek city of Ephesus (the play's setting) and the Sicilian city of Syracuse (Egeon's home). Still mourning the loss of his family these many years after their tragic separation, he welcomes death, and his tale of woe so moves the Duke of Ephesus that Egeon is given a day to gather one thousand marks to ransom his life and be freed.

The slapstick and humor of *The Comedy of Errors* is on full display when we learn that the younger Antipholus and Dromio have also recently arrived in Ephesus, and that the older Antipholus and Dromio have lived there since the time of their rescue at sea. The older Antipholus is a married, well-respected, wealthy merchant and his attendant Dromio is engaged to Antipholus's cook. The younger Antipholus and Dromio are traveling merchants trying to maintain a low profile, lest anyone find out that they are also from Syracuse. These circumstances set the stage for a hilarious cascade of misunderstandings.

The saucy wordplay, Punch and Judy–style buffoonery, pranks, jokes, and wry sarcasm of the Dromio twins make *The Comedy of Errors* a wild and silly farce. Mistaken identity is taken to an absurdly comedic level: one of the storylines revolves around the older Antipholus being late for dinner, his younger brother being mistaken for him and forced to dine with his wife, and then the older Antipholus being locked out of his own home at suppertime so as not to disturb his wife and the man she thinks is her husband. The clownish transfer of various props, such as a pouch of money, a rope, a gold chain, and a key add to the hilarity. These props circulate back and forth among the Antipholus and Dromio twins, wreaking havoc on their relationships as each is confounded by the person they wrongly believe to be their lifelong companion.

Various dinner invitations are exchanged, unusual behaviors are accommodated, sacrifices are made, and the uproarious events of the day lead everyone to an abbey, behind which Egeon is to be executed. Emilia makes a surprise appearance in the final scene as head abbess, joyfully reuniting her husband and sons in the same room for the first time that day (and for the first time in twenty years). The hullabaloo of the day's events, involving money, gold chains, ransom, and a dinner gone cold, is soon forgotten upon the family's reunion.

In times of great difficulty, the opportunity to come together and have a few laughs with friends and family is a heavenly respite. Remember how much you looked forward to a simple meal around a table when the COVID-19 lockdown restrictions were lifted? Londoners in the Elizabethan era felt the same way, and Shakespeare's plays were often part of the celebration. The Plague Orders of 1578 required the subjects of the realm to quarantine, wash and/or burn infected bedding, lay out their dead in designated areas, avoid social gatherings, and receive food and drink from appointed suppliers. As the orders were periodically lifted between outbreaks of contagion, Londoners came out to celebrate, often by attending a play.

The Comedy of Errors, one of Shakespeare's earliest known plays, was performed as part of the Christmas holiday revels on December 28, 1594, at Gray's Inn, one of London's four Inns of Court. The winter revels sometimes lasted from November to February, a time when the resident law students and barrister society members celebrated with singing, dancing, theatrical performances, mock trials, the election of an honorary ruler called the Prince of Purpoole, and satirical speeches and debates. These holiday revels may be the precursor to the American tradition of annual "law school follies," where barristers in training parody and celebrate their chosen careers and the state of the state.

During the Christmas revels, the law students welcomed back alumni and invited the country's supreme mother, Queen

12   **Shakespeare's Guide to Living the Good Life**

Elizabeth I, to participate in the celebrations. It is fitting that this festive comedy featuring parents and children, separation, reunion, and hospitality was first performed in a time and place where those themes were being played out in real life.

The first live performance I saw of *The Comedy of Errors* was enacted for a group of kindergarteners and first graders. The slapstick comedy, the wild, flailing use of props, and the acrobatic antics of the actors delighted the young children, who had no problem following the storyline or understanding the humor. They laughed out loud, squealed with glee, and tried in vain to help the Antipholuses and Dromios solve their comic dilemmas.

This is exactly how a Shakespeare comedy is meant to be—interactive, mirthful, and entertaining for young and old alike. In fact, this play has the farcical feel of a Saturday morning cartoon where the mouse has conjured twenty-seven ways to play tricks on the cat, and the audience is in on the joke. Full of horseplay and hijinks, *The Comedy of Errors* reminds us of the humor inherent in life.

The Comedy of Errors is a perfect example of the absurd shenanigans that comprised sixteenth-century Elizabethan theater, which provided a few hours of escapism during dark times. As waves of bubonic plague swept through the populace every few years from 1348 to 1679, it's no surprise that audiences craved the opportunity to laugh, if only to keep from crying.

Hospitality

This play points to deeper truths about what it means to be human as well. Human beings are complex creatures, capable of feeling multiple emotions simultaneously. Comedy is often the result of our ability to embody the polarity that permeates our human existence; finding humor in the midst of extreme sadness is what we do, and the benefits can be tremendously healing. While the bard's thrust here is comedy, we can also sympathize with the pain associated with separation from one's family, whether by pandemic-imposed isolation, children going off to college, deployment, or loss of a loved one.

Laughter has tremendous power to heal the pain of loss and separation, particularly when that pain has reached a boiling point. We know that laughter releases tension, lowers blood pressure, reduces pain, and even improves immunity.[1] When tension and stress are at a peak, the healing power of laughter is most potent, like the release valve on a pressure cooker. In our darkest moments, Shakespeare is inviting us to laugh and even play.

Shakespeare and his thespian colleagues used their many talents to delight, regale, distract, comfort, and amuse their audiences. It was a respite from the dreary and often terrifying times they lived in, not knowing when another round of the plague would blow into town and take away their loved ones on its way out. (The plague was such an ever-present part of life in England during Shakespeare's time that the children's nursery rhyme "Ring Around the Rosie" is said to have originally referred to the plague.) Shakespeare and his pals offered an opportunity for playgoers to release the valve on the pressure cooker by spending time together and sharing a laugh.

Our lives in the twenty-first century are eerily similar to those of Shakespeare's audience, who must have thought that death lurked around every corner. We doomscroll, obsess, panic, and take things so seriously that our runaway worries exacerbate the sadness. Left to our own devices, we amplify our fears until they take on a life of their own, one that is quite different from reality. In those cases, the only way out is to take a step back and laugh at ourselves. That's what Shakespeare offers us in *The Comedy of Errors*, reminding us to be silly, and not to take our gold chains, pouches of money, ropes, and keys too seriously. Will and his pals offered a form of community at the theater that was desperately needed—a gathering place, a warm welcome, and a few hours to shake off the feeling of malaise. That kind of hospitality focuses more on the feeling of being together than the accoutrements or décor.

When my partner and I moved into our tiny house a few years ago, it (and we) came with nothing. No beds, no couch, no tables or chairs, no rugs. We didn't have dishes or cutlery and were drinking everything out of travel beverage tumblers. A few of our closest family members wanted to see our new place, which mortified us, because, to use Shakespeare's terminology, our tiny home boasted the smallest "cheer" known to humankind. In some ways we were like the twin Antipholuses

Hospitality   15

and Dromios—out of sorts, separated from our familiar surroundings, and living in an alternate reality. Our family members asserted that being together was more important than having a comfortable bed or proper dinnerware, so, like the characters in *The Comedy of Errors*, we went with the flow: "I'll say as they say, and persever so, and in this mist at all adventures go." We told them to bring sleeping bags and camping gear, and we'd do our best to offer a great welcome.

It was January, and our only source of heat was a wood-burning fireplace in the living room. We ordered pizza, sat on the floor, drank wine out of mugs, begged some firewood from a new neighbor, and lined up our bedrolls in a row in front of the hearth. It didn't matter that we were without the traditional trappings of hospitality—our bizarre circumstances felt exciting and special. We relived our favorite camping trips, wondered if this was how our ancestors had lived hundreds of years ago, felt proud of ourselves for roughing it, and made memories that we will never forget.

The separation that Duke Egeon's family suffers in *The Comedy of Errors* is all too familiar to those of us who endured the social distancing and isolation of the COVID-19 pandemic. Duke Egeon's family members find themselves on opposite sides of a ship's mast when the wooden beam splits in two, and many families during the pandemic found themselves similarly split apart. Separated geographically, or by medical conditions that prohibited us from being together, we were

16   **Shakespeare's Guide to Living the Good Life**

isolated from our families and friends, and were forced to deal with the waves of loneliness and uncertainty.

The distress that many experienced under confinement was not simply a vague feeling of unrest. Scientific studies have shown that psychological disorders such as anxiety and panic, obsessive-compulsive symptoms, insomnia, digestive problems, as well as depressive symptoms and post-traumatic stress are exacerbated by social isolation.[2] The World Health Organization reported in 2022 that the global prevalence of anxiety and depression increased by an extraordinary 25 percent in one year as a result of the COVID-19 pandemic.[3] According to a recent National Institutes of Health report, severe loneliness increased by 350 percent in the first year of the pandemic, as compared to prior to COVID-19.[4]

Even before the pandemic, researchers were growing concerned over the long-term effects of isolation and loneliness. The results show that an objective lack of interaction has a profound negative effect on our well-being, including cardiovascular and mental health conditions.[5] For example, researchers found that social isolation and loneliness increase the risk of having a heart attack by 29 percent and the risk of having a stroke by 32 percent. The report also showed that a lack of social connection was associated with increased risk of premature death from all causes, especially among men. The five-year heart failure survival rate for people who were socially isolated

Hospitality

was only 60 percent—much lower than for those who had established social contacts.[6]

Human beings need contact with each other, and the hugging and handshaking that accompany time together—whether hanging out at your child's soccer game or dance recital, or inviting a few friends over for dinner—have a calming effect on all of us. Other studies have shown that those who eat socially more often feel happier and are more satisfied with life, are more trusting of others, are more engaged with their local communities, and have more friends they can depend on for support.[7] These studies demonstrate the positive physical manifestations of connecting with other human beings, of living in community, which is the way we have lived for thousands of years. But when our connections are severed, our social routines upended, we suffer. This is exactly what happens to the estranged family in *The Comedy of Errors*. They are living in chaos and a feeling of altered reality, much like the surreal experience we felt during the pandemic.

Priests baptizing babies with a (holy) water pistol from six feet away. A Michelin-starred restaurant giving away a free roll of toilet paper with each carry-out order of chicken pâté en croute. Packs of jackals, mountain goats, and wild boars taking over the local playgrounds and parks. A world-renowned string quartet performing at a Barcelona opera house before an audience comprised solely of two thousand live plants. The internet is rife with examples of the surreal events during the

18   Shakespeare's Guide to Living the Good Life

peak of the pandemic. In many ways, the last few years have been their own comedy of errors—and suddenly the bizarre actions of Shakespeare's wacky protagonists don't seem so odd after all.

Consider Shakespeare's take on isolation, as demonstrated by Antipholus's expression of loneliness and grief over the separation from his brother and mother:

> He that commends me to mine own content
> commends me to the thing I cannot get.
> I to the world am like a drop of water
> that in the ocean seeks another drop,
> who, falling there to find his fellow forth,
> unseen, inquisitive, confounds himself.
> So I, to find a mother and a brother,
> in quest of them, unhappy, lose myself.
> (*The Comedy of Errors*, act 1, scene 2)

Separation from our friends and family can take us to the brink of desperation, where our old identities, like Antipholus, are lost. Those of us who are self-proclaimed introverts might seek solitary time to recharge, but we also thrive in an environment that includes a few close friends and good conversation, possibly around a firepit, a kitchen table, or on the front steps. Whether you are a quiet-loving introvert or a party-going extrovert, the desire to be seen and heard is universal. It

Hospitality

is the real human connection that we make with others when we gather, wherever that may be, that feeds our souls, reminding us that we are all connected. Shakespeare understood the importance of gathering, as evidenced by the following scene, in which Antipholus is inviting his friend, Balthasar, to dinner, and the two debate whether it is the food or the company that makes for the best hospitality:

> ANTIPHOLUS (E)
> You're sad, Signior Balthasar. Pray God our cheer
> may answer my goodwill and your good welcome here.
>
> BALTHASAR
> I hold your dainties cheap, sir, and your welcome dear.
>
> ANTIPHOLUS (E)
> O Signior Balthasar, either at flesh or fish
> a table full of welcome makes scarce one dainty dish.
>
> BALTHASAR
> Good meat, sir, is common; that every churl affords.
>
> ANTIPHOLUS (E)
> And welcome more common, for that's nothing more
>   than words. . . .
> But though my cates be mean, take them in good part.
> Better cheer may you have, but not with better heart.
> (*The Comedy of Errors*, act 3, scene 1)

Shakespeare comes out squarely on the side of company, rather than food, as the method by which hospitality boosts our sense of well-being. I've always interpreted that to mean that being together is more important than an immaculate tablescape or a crumb-free kitchen counter.

Hospitality derives from the Latin *hospitalitem*, which means "friendliness to guests." Interestingly, the Latin word for "guest" is *hospes*, which also means "stranger, sojourner, or visitor." In this context, offering hospitality includes offering friendliness to strangers. It is clear that William Shakespeare understood the origin of the word *hospitality* and took it to a comedic extreme in exploring the offer of "friendliness to guests" who were strangers.

The Bible also extols the virtues of hospitality, as in this verse from Saint Paul's letter to the Romans: "When God's people are in need, be ready to help them. Always be eager to practice hospitality" (Romans 12:13). Paul's letter was a plea to the Christian church in Rome to be kind and welcome everyone in need, which he identified as offering hospitality. At the time of Paul's epistle, there were ongoing disputes between Rome's Jewish population and the early Christian gentile church. Paul was advising the early Christians to help anyone in need, regardless of whether they shared the same faith. That is the nature of hospitality.

One of the most intriguing definitions of hospitality is offered by eighteenth-century physician and philosopher Louis, Chevalier de Jaucourt. He was the most prolific contributor to the French Enlightenment's *Encyclopédie*, a compendium of information intended to provide insights on art, science, philosophy, history, and politics, published in 1765. In the *Encyclopédie,* Louis de Jaucourt describes hospitality as "the virtue of a great soul that cares for the whole universe through the ties of humanity." Jaucourt's entry on hospitality continues, "The Stoics regarded it as a duty inspired by God himself. One must, they said, do good to people who come to our countries, less for their sake than for our own interest, for the sake of virtue and in order to perfect in our souls human sentiments, which must not be limited to the ties of blood and friendship, but extended to all mortals." This definition is more of a "love your neighbor as yourself" kind of hospitality that is particularly apposite in modern times, where extreme weather and political unrest have decimated certain parts of the world. Our displaced brothers and sisters are in desperate need of the kindness, support, and benevolence demonstrated by the characters in *The Comedy of Errors.* Our offerings of welcome and cheer are an integral part of living the good life. Given the current state of the world, this version of hospitality on a broader, more global basis is an appealing notion—one with which Shakespeare certainly agrees.

Enactments

The following enactments are designed to help you incorporate Shakespeare's hospitality into your own life. Get ready to gather your friends and loved ones!

Make a Merry Feast

In Shakespeare's time, the master of the revels had one of the most entertaining jobs in the world: creating the fun. We can do the same today by throwing a celebratory feast of our own. In *The Comedy of Errors*, Shakespeare reminds us that the merry feast is less about the venue, decorations, and food (the *cheer*) and more about the genuine goodwill and warmheartedness of the hosts (the *welcome*): "Small cheer and great welcome makes a merry feast." By keeping it simple and remembering what is most important, throwing a feast can be a fun and easy way to enjoy the best of hospitality.

If you aren't in the habit of hosting dinner parties for friends or family, you might try having a potluck to start, with each person contributing a part of the meal. This eases the potential financial burden and the stress of feeding a large group. Or you could try organizing a supper club with friends or neighbors, where you each take turns hosting a meal once a month. Impromptu add-ons and plus-ones during the holidays are also great opportunities to practice hospitality and openness. I can assure you that while your surprise guest(s) may not remember the specific food they were served, they will surely not forget having a gracious and thoughtful host.

Happy Memory Jar Game

Studies have shown that consciously recalling positive events from your life can prevent depression, boost happiness, and increase longevity—and when you do this practice with your friends, partner, family, or neighbors, it strengthens social bonds. By sharing these memories, we call forth the best of ourselves, as Dromio and Antipholus do when Egeon first sees them after twenty years apart: "Ourselves we do remember, sir, by you." One way to consciously deepen your connection to positive recollections is to create a happy memory jar.

At your next family holiday, neighborhood block party, or high school reunion—or near the end of an event such as a camping trip or retreat—put out a mason jar, a few pens, and some slips of paper. Ask everyone to write down two or three favorite memories, fold the slips of paper, and add them to the jar anonymously. When everyone has contributed at least one memory to the jar, gather in a circle and pass the jar around, allowing each person to read one memory out loud to the group. The group can then guess who wrote the memory, and when correctly identified you can add the person's name to it. In some cases, the author will be easy to identify—in others, not so much. Participants are often surprised as to who a particular memory belongs to. But in all cases, notice the shared laughter, the embellishments, and the reminiscing among all members of the group, who are now creating *more* memories by participating in the sharing circle.

You can also play the memory jar game in honor of a specific person—for example, at their birthday, graduation, or retirement party. For this variation, circulate the jar to each person present, asking them to contribute a positive memory involving the guest of honor, and again, without signing it. At the end of the event, take the time to read every memory out loud, allowing each positive memory to trigger other memories in an expanding circle of joy, and guessing who contributed the memory, adding their name to it. Return the memories to the jar and present it to the honoree as a gift to mark the occasion.

Lastly, consider playing this game at the reception after a funeral, honoring the one who has passed. This may allow the group to bring laughter and joy to a sorrowful occasion, remembering their best memories of the deceased. Once all memories have been read and the authorship identified, return the memories to the jar and offer it as a gift to the deceased's family members. The jar may serve as a comfort to them, a collection of stories that's available anytime they are feeling down or missing their loved one.

Express Your Appreciation

Another method for creating a great welcome, à la *The Comedy of Errors*, is to show someone how genuinely thrilled you are to have them in your life. Think of the way a dog greets its human when they walk in the front door. There is no greater mood booster, and it's based on the simple premise that we are truly ecstatic to be reunited with those we love (especially if they have been separated from us for some time). Emilia, the mother of the double set of twins in *The Comedy of Errors*, is so ecstatic to see her family together under one roof after so many years apart that she likens it to them being born to her all over again:

The Duke, my husband, and my children both,
and you the calendars of their nativity,
go to a gossips' feast [baptism celebration], and go with me.
After so long grief, such nativity!
(*The Comedy of Errors*, act 5, scene 1)

Employ your preferred love language (words of affirmation, acts of service, physical touch, gift-giving, quality time, and so on) and take the time to express your appreciation for the important people in your life. What if we all greeted each other with the enthusiasm our pets show us every time we walk into a room? We have the power to create those feelings of genuine affection, warmth, connection, belonging, and love in each other. Shakespeare encourages us to use it.

Chapter Two

Imagination

A Midsummer Night's Dream

A Midsummer Night's Dream begins four days prior to the wedding of Athenian King Theseus to Amazonian Queen Hippolyta. As they prepare for their nuptial celebration, a nobleman named Egeus requests that Theseus force Egeus's daughter, Hermia, to marry young lord Demetrius. Hermia, who is in love with Lysander, balks at the request, and Lysander jumps in to argue for her hand, to no avail. King Theseus offers Hermia the options of death, marriage to Demetrius, or life in a convent. Hermia prefers death or a nunnery over marriage to Demetrius, and Theseus gives her twenty-four hours to change her mind. Lysander reveals to Hermia that he has a wealthy widowed aunt who lives beyond Theseus's jurisdiction; she has promised to harbor the young couple and leave her fortune to them in her will. Hermia is thrilled and they plan to leave that night.

Hermia divulges her plans to Helena, expecting that the latter will welcome the news; Demetrius recently dumped Helena for Hermia. Helena reveals the plan to Demetrius, hoping he will come to his senses and take her back. He doesn't; instead, he takes off into the woods to find Hermia with Helena tagging behind, bemoaning the failure of her quixotic plan.

In the forest, Hermia instructs Lysander to sleep away from her to protect her chastity until their marriage. They plan to travel to the home of Lysander's aunt in the morning.

In the same enchanted wood, Fairy King Oberon and Fairy Queen Titania are quarreling over the queen's new ward, a young orphan boy who entered Titania's care after his mother's death. Oberon is so jealous that he plots to send the boy away, and Titania enjoys playing with her husband's emotions. Oberon instructs the wily Robin Goodfellow (aka "Puck") to find Eros's flower and press the juice onto Titania's eyes as she sleeps, such that the first thing she sees when she wakes, "be it on lion, bear, on wolf, or bull, or meddling monkey, or on busy ape" will infatuate her with lust. While she is distracted, Oberon plans to remove her page and teach his fairy wife a lesson about toying with the king.

The wood becomes disturbed by the fairy dispute and the complaints of the disgruntled lovers. Adding to the chaos is a rag-tag band of trade workers-cum-actors who utilize the forest as their rehearsal space for a performance scheduled for Theseus and Hippolyta's marriage celebration. The weaver, Nick Bottom, the most boisterous and uninhibited of the players, wants to play all the parts. The exasperated director/carpenter, Peter Quince,

Shakespeare's Guide to Living the Good Life

denies Bottom's request, so Bottom instead doles out unsolicited advice to the other actors on how to play their parts.

Puck spies the "hempen homespuns" practicing their play and as instructed by Oberon, Puck turns Bottom into a donkey for Titania to lust after. The actors return, see the monstrous "asshead" Bottom, and run away. His friends tell Bottom that he has become a beast, but Bottom believes they are trying to scare him in the dark wood, so he sings to keep from being frightened. His song wakes Titania, who immediately falls in love with him. They enjoy an evening of lovemaking and Oberon steals Titania's young ward.

Oberon sees Helena in the forest and is sympathetic to her plight. The fairy king directs Puck to press Eros's same flower juice onto the sleeping Demetrius, whom Oberon calls "the Athenian," so that when he wakes, he will fall in love with Helena.

Puck, who doesn't know there are multiple Athenians in the wood, mistakenly presses the juice into Lysander's eyes, and because Hermia has distanced herself far away from him, Lysander falls in love with Helena when he wakes. The chaos in the wood is now amplified: Helena sobs loudly that she is being mocked by Lysander, Hermia questions why her lover has tossed her over, Lysander tussles with Demetrius to get to Helena, and Demetrius tries to make sense of the nonsense. After much comedic hand-wringing, shouting, and waggery, Oberon chastises Puck and directs him to set things aright.

Puck enchants each person back to sleep, applies the love potion antidote to Titania and Lysander, drops the Eros flower

Imagination   29

juice in Demetrius's eyes, and situates Helena within arm's reach of him. The four lovers awaken as Hippolyta, Theseus, and their morning hunting party enter the wood. Demetrius surprises everyone when he withdraws his offer of marriage to Hermia, requesting instead to marry Helena. Theseus blesses the marriage of Helena to Demetrius and Hermia to Lysander, and they all return to court to celebrate three weddings.

At the wedding feast in Athens, Bottom is still missing and the actors fear that King Theseus will have them hanged for a piss-poor stage play attempted without their star actor. Bottom magically appears at the last minute, so inspired by his liaison with the fairy queen that he puts on a stellar performance. The fairy king and queen resolve their differences, and all the fairies wing their way from the wood to the court to offer their blessings for the marriage:

Hand in hand, with fairy grace,
will we sing and bless this place.
(*A Midsummer Night's Dream*, act 5, scene 1)

Shakespeare knew that when the external world is full of chaos and turmoil, an afternoon or evening filled with fairies, fantasy, forest, flowers, and frolicking is a welcome respite.

The Elizabethans were enamored of all things astrological, supernatural, mythical, and historical, and Plutarch's *Lives of the Noble Grecians and Romans*, finally translated into English by Thomas North in 1579, was all the rage with the 30 percent of the population who could read. Plutarch includes an intriguing story of Theseus's war with the fierce community of female warriors known as the Amazons, which must have pleased Queen Elizabeth I and her contemporaries immensely. Plutarch recounts that after three months of fighting with no definitive victor, the Amazonian Queen, Hippolyta, negotiated a peace treaty with Theseus. The war-ending accord was sealed by their marriage.

Hippolyta's marriage to Theseus is the subject of *A Midsummer Night's Dream*, one of Shakespeare's funniest and most popular plays, and one which provides not only Greek mythology and historical subject matter but also a bit of England's own magical folklore, embodied in Robin "Puck" Goodfellow. Even if you've never seen a Shakespeare play, you probably know all about the "shrewd and knavish" hobgoblin Puck, who has become so popular in modern culture that his name is used as an adjective to describe good-hearted yet chaos-causing behavior.

Most scholars agree that this play was written sometime between 1594 and 1596. At this time, Shakespeare was not the revered national poet of England, but rather a working-class actor drawing from his daily experiences to eke out a

Imagination

living as a traveling writer/performer. Many wealthy aristocrats commissioned marriage-themed plays or performances as part of high society wedding celebrations. Acting companies who were well received could expect to be in demand, thus guaranteeing a somewhat steady paycheck.

In fact, many scholars believe that *A Midsummer Night's Dream* was written to be performed for the marriage of Thomas Heneage and the Countess of Southampton in May 1594, only to be revised nearly two years later for the marriage of Elizabeth Carey and Thomas Berkley. Neither version included the charming epilogue offered by Puck as published in the first quarto of 1600. This puts a different spin on Shakespeare the writer—not an otherworldly magician who easily spewed out literary genius from his quill onto the page, but a working member of a theatre company on a deadline, taking inspiration from his surroundings, and adapting his works over time through trial and error, with the benefit of private performances and audience reactions to help him refine his finished product.

The first live performance I saw of *A Midsummer Night's Dream* was outdoors, "Shakespeare in the Park" style, a most fitting location to soak up the atmosphere of this pastoral comedy. We laid out our picnic blankets and chairs as the sun dipped behind the noble and swaying pines, whose quiet murmurs mixed with ours as we whispered in eager anticipation. The "stage" was a portable wooden dance floor laid on the ground, and the actors took their places just a few paces from our seats on the grass. Several cast members played acoustic instruments, and the music floated into the air as if carried by the fairies themselves. The birds twittered from the branches, and it felt like the woods and glade had appeared there like magic to commune with Titania, Oberon, Puck, and Bottom. I had the fleeting feeling that if I returned the next day, it would all be gone. As I was overwhelmed by the beauty of the twilight meadow and thinking it couldn't be more perfect, the evening's first fireflies emerged, dancing around the fairy king and queen as if they were part of the cast (as far as I'm concerned, they were).

The ethereal quality of the play evokes a feeling that the audience is dreaming along with Titania and the Athenians throughout the night. The fact that the dreaming takes place in the wood also calls forth the wonder of nature, including the shadowy effects of the moonlight playing among the tree branches, mist rising off the water, and the sounds of woodland creatures echoing throughout the space. This little taste of spritely magic is extraordinary in its intimacy:

And I serve the fairy queen,
to dew her orbs upon the green.
The cowslips tall her pensioners be:
in their gold coats spots you see;
those be rubies, fairy favors,

Imagination

in those freckles live their savors:

I must go seek some dewdrops here

and hang a pearl in every cowslip's ear.

(*A Midsummer Night's Dream*, act 2, scene 1)

Shakespeare invites us to let go of the ordinary and lean into the unexpected, which is exactly what happens when we dream. We often have experiences that we can't explain, travel to places that we've never been, and interact with people and things we've never met. This trip to the subconscious brings with it revelations and changes in perspective that inspire us to move our lives forward. We can imagine ourselves as Nick Bottom, a weaver of threads by day and a weaver of stories by night. How would we feel if we found ourselves in the fairy queen's open-air boudoir, surrounded by her attendants Mustardseed, Cobweb, Moth, and Peaseblossom, magical pixies who cater to our every whim? How would we be inspired and affected?

The strict and harsh rules of the Athenian court in the beginning of the play are worlds away from the mystical beauty of the woodland dreamworld, much like our own dreams are worlds apart from our quotidian obligations. Hermia is forced to obey her father's will, and Lysander feels powerless to follow his heart. Helena has been tossed aside by Demetrius without a care. Theseus's impending marriage is based on the need to secure a peace treaty that will avoid future conflicts with the Amazonian warriors. The Athens of *A Midsummer Night's Dream* is not too far afield from our own lives.

Theseus's exposition on the law, as explained to Hermia, tells us everything we need to know about the Elizabethans' view of world structure:

> To you, your father should be as a god,
> one that composed your beauties, yea, and one
> to whom you are but as a form in wax
> by him imprinted, and within his power
> to leave the figure or disfigure it.
> (*A Midsummer Night's Dream*, act 1, scene 1)

The play's acting troupe, whom Puck labels "rude mechanicals," are struggling when we meet them in the city—they are anxious to please the king, worried whether they've chosen the right play, and bickering about which actor should play each part. Yes, they are actors and thus creative artists, but we know that this is their side hustle because by day they are construction and trade workers, working long hours at backbreaking physical labor. The theater and the world of imagination are their refuge from the harsh reality of their difficult lives.

It's not until the characters enter the misty woodland after moonrise (a symbol of the imagination) that they transcend the limitations of their daily lives. Like the characters in *A Midsummer Night's Dream*, we escape the restrictions put upon us only when we take ourselves out of the routine and into our own imaginations. I've often wondered whether Shakespeare himself struggled over a couplet or a scene that eluded him, only to find that after a good night's sleep the words flowed easily. The oneiric experience loosens the dam formed by the daily grind and releases the creative flow.

Anecdotal evidence abounds about the transformative power of dreams. The number of researchers and artists throughout history who have attributed breakthroughs to solutions that appeared in dreams is staggering. A few examples: Dmitri Mendeleev credited a dream with the creation of the periodic table of chemical elements; August Kekulé couldn't figure out the structure of benzene atoms until he dreamed of a snake made of atoms eating its tail and realized that benzene atoms are in the shape of a carbon ring; and René Descartes recalled a dream on November 10, 1619, which gave him the framework for the scientific method.

And from the world of the creative arts: Paul McCartney woke up from a dream with a tune in his head and wrote the song "Yesterday"; Gordon "Sting" Sumner composed "Every Breath You Take" on the piano in the middle of the night after waking up from a dream with the lyrics in his head; Michael Stipe dreamed he went to a party with Leonard Bernstein, Leonid Brezhnev, Lenny Bruce, and Lester Bangs, where they ate birthday cake and jelly beans, and wrote "It's the End of the World As We Know It (And I Feel Fine)"; and Johnny

Cash had a dream in which mariachi horns were playing over a song he was preparing to record, entitled "Ring of Fire."

One of the most magical experiences I had was several years ago when my family celebrated the summer solstice at Stonehenge with ten thousand other revelers, including druids, naturalists, mystics, hippies, and tourists from all over the world. We arrived at 2:00 a.m. and walked in darkness around the sacred grounds on Salisbury Plain, where people were already celebrating with dancing, music, and all manner of esoteric rituals. Sunrise was at 4:41 a.m., and a hush came over the crowd as we awaited the arrival of Apollo's golden chariot. Imagining that ancient celebrants were witnessing the same thing over five thousand years before on this very ground brought me to tears.

The stones were humming, and not from the drums beating, but from within the earth, an electric buzzing that I had never felt before. As I raised my right hand to place it on one of the massive standing sarsens, a woman in a brightly colored skirt, tank top, bare feet, and dirty blond dreadlocks grabbed my hand and pushed it toward the ground. "No, not that one—use your left hand—only then will you perceive what the stones have to offer," she said. Confused but thankful for the advice, I held my left hand up to the stone and felt the hum of the stones reverberate throughout my body. It felt like being charged up, as if I were a battery that didn't even realize it was drained. Everyone in our family tried it, and we all

Imagination   37

felt a similar wave of exuberance and contentment. We think about that trip often, and when I remember the vibration that transferred from the earth to the stones and into my body through my outstretched hand, it reminds me that there is untold magic in the world.

Many studies have been conducted regarding changes that occur in the brain during and after we have experienced a dream state or a new positive experience. Studies show that dreaming, whether as part of a full night's sleep or a mid-afternoon nap (including REM sleep), improves memory and problem-solving abilities.[1] In one study, participants were shown how to navigate a maze, and then one group took a scheduled nap for the same amount of time that the control group watched a related video. Both groups were asked to navigate the maze again. The group that had napped experienced significantly improved performance, even though the group that stayed awake watched a task-related video. The researchers concluded that dreaming was immensely beneficial for the problem-solving components of memory because those memories are consolidated and activated when we sleep.[2]

In addition to problem-solving, imagination and dreams have a significant effect on emotional regulation. Many studies confirm that dreaming is essential for our ability to respond to emotional events in our lives. For example, a study was conducted with participants whose dream sleep was interrupted for the same amount of time that the control group's non-dream sleep was interrupted. Those who were deprived of dream sleep suffered from a diminished capacity to cope with emotional events.[3]

The characters in *A Midsummer Night's Dream* undergo some of the most traumatic emotional experiences that humans can endure. Hermia, a feisty young woman in love with Lysander, is prohibited by both her father and the laws of Athens from marrying him. The lack of personal sovereignty, injustice, and anguish inherent in her situation is relatable in the modern world, where we feel like our voices are not heard, our choices are not our own, and we are governed by rules we didn't make. Hermia's choices under Athenian law are: (1) marriage to Demetrius; (2) austerity in a convent; or (3) death. If anyone needs a problem-solving dream sleep, it's Hermia.

Similarly, Helena inhabits her own hell, in that Demetrius courts her and wins her heart, then throws her over for Hermia like yesterday's smelly stockings. When Helena sees an opportunity to win back Demetrius's love, her tattling backfires, and Demetrius's treatment of Helena moves from indifferent to cruel: "Tempt not too much the hatred of my spirit, for I am sick when I do look on thee." Ouch.

The fairy queen, Titania, is embroiled in conflict as well, caught between her own show of sovereignty and her love for Oberon. When she retires to her bed that night, her flock of fairy attendants sings her to sleep with a soothing lullaby to induce good dreams:

Philomel, with melody

sing in our sweet lullaby.

lulla, lulla, lullaby, lulla, lulla, lullaby.

never harm

nor spell nor charm

come our lovely lady nigh.

So good night, with lullaby.

(*A Midsummer Night's Dream*, act 2, scene 2)

The Athenian lovers, the fairy queen, and Nick Bottom do not know what to expect when they enter into the world of dreams and imagination, but they all have anxieties and issues created by their relationships. Through the course of the evening, thanks to mischief, trickery, and the misguided hijinks of the hobgoblin, Puck, they awake from their dreams with solutions they didn't expect. In this, Shakespeare's whimsical nuptial comedy, the night's dreams are made more extraordinary through the mischief of fairies, but using our imagination works just as well for us, even without the assistance of elves and fay.

Enactments

The magic of dreams isn't just reserved for nighttime! Use your imagination to bring the enchanting world of *A Midsummer Night's Dream* to life with the following enactments.

Camp in the Yard

This enactment is fantastically fun if you have young children, but even if your children are older and think they have grown beyond this kind of expedition, give it a try—it might rekindle the magic of childhood in everyone.

Put up a tent in your yard, bring out the sleeping bags, hang a few lanterns, spread a blanket with simple, no-cook food, and get cozy. As the stars appear in the sky, take the time to look for planets like Venus, Mercury, Mars, or Jupiter, and see if you can pick out any constellations. There are free smartphone apps that can help with identifying the celestial sights, and it's fun to see if you can make out the shapes of the constellations. If you have access to a firepit, or a few tiki torches, toast some marshmallows and notice how your own yard looks different in the flickering lights under the night sky. Take turns making up stories about your camping adventure. Are you in a medieval forest filled with fairies, pixies, brownies, and leprechauns? Or are you soldiers making camp on your way to an epic battle? Or maybe you live in the wild and can talk to the animals. Are you magicians like Oberon or enchanted spirits like Puck? Add to each other's stories and write them down—maybe they will become a book one day!

Recall Enchanting Times and Places

Certain times of the year and locations we've visited hold magical memories. Taking the time to recall and consider what

Imagination 41

makes those times and places so enchanting is a wonderful enactment that not only brings to mind meaningful experiences, but also helps us to understand where the magic in our lives exists.

Whatever season you are in when you read this book, what is your favorite part of this season? Write it down. For example, as I write this chapter, it is Ren Faire season in many areas of the United States. Surprise, surprise—this is one of my favorite magical times! Are there festivals, celebrations, vacations, or happenings that you enjoy at different times of the year? Do you participate in them every year, and look forward to them coming around again? Write down what they are, why they are important to you, and the characteristics that make them special.

Have you ever visited a place and felt like you were in a completely different reality? For some, this might be a trip to the beach, a hike in the mountains, or a cabin near the lake. What draws you to these places? Do they feel magical to you? Compare places like this that you visit alone (such as a local pond or hiking trail) to those that you share with friends and family. How are they different? How do these spaces speak to you and inform your imagination?

Surprise a Loved One with the Stuff of Dreams

We are all magicians in our own right, and we can use our imaginations to create magical experiences for the special people in our lives. Think about what you would like to create for someone special. Here are some suggestions.

Make a musical playlist to set the magical mood, and gather some twinkling lights or glow-in-the-dark beads. Drive to a park or a high point where you can sit back and watch the stars. Bring flowers and your favorite beverage, and invite the magic into the evening, surprising your special someone with their own mystic night's dream.

Plan an evening where you make your special someone's favorite food, and decorate the room to evoke the feeling of that food's origin. If they are Shakespeare enthusiasts, make a playlist of Elizabethan recorder music, hang some ornamental tapestries, fill the space with pillar and taper candles, and decorate with traditional Tudor roses. Make shepherd's pie, savory tarts, and custard for dessert. If you can memorize a few lines of Shakespeare to recite to your loved one, you will have created a magical moment that will not soon be forgotten.

Plan a surprise trip for your special someone to a place they've always wanted to go. Treat them like a king or queen, taking care of every detail and making the event momentous. If they like the theater or a particular musical performer, buy tickets to a show, dress up, make or take them to a special dinner, and celebrate them as a guest of honor and VIP for the entire event. Use your imagination to make a dream come true.

Chapter Three

Compassion
The Merchant of Venice

The play begins in Venice with friends Antonio and Bassanio discussing the virtues of a young woman in Belmont, Italy:

> Her name is Portia, nothing undervalued
> to Cato's daughter, Brutus' Portia,
> nor is the wide world ignorant of her worth
> for the four winds blow in from every coast
> renownèd suitors, and her sunny locks
> hang on her temples like a golden fleece,
> which makes her seat of Belmont Colchos' strond,
> and many Jasons come in quest of her.
> (*The Merchant of Venice*, act 1, scene 1)

Shakespeare paints the picture early on that Portia is equivalent to a Greek goddess. Despite her many virtues, she is pinioned and powerless, treated like a piece of property in her recently deceased father's will, which states that she must marry the suitor who chooses the correct treasure chest from a choice of three: gold, silver, and lead.

Bassanio seeks to become a suitor, but the will requires payment of a fee for the opportunity to choose a casket. Bassanio's Venetian friend Antonio obtains a loan from the local moneylender Shylock to pay the fee on credit. However, Antonio's merchant ships are still at sea, which renders him unable to provide collateral for the loan. Shylock, who has been poorly treated by Antonio in the past, suggests as a "kindness," and (Antonio believes) a joke, that Antonio pledge a pound of his "fair flesh" as bond for the loan. If the loan is not repaid by the deadline, the bond gives Shylock the right to slice off a pound of Antonio's flesh "in what part of [his] body pleaseth [Shylock]."

Meanwhile, in Belmont, Portia anxiously observes the suitors as they select the caskets, all the while wishing that she could make her own decision and marry Bassanio, whom she had met and fallen in love with some time ago. The Prince of Morocco chooses the gold casket, which is incorrect, and which bears a scroll with the message that "all that glisters is not gold," meaning that he who judges solely by outside appearances judges wrongly. The Prince of Arragon chooses the silver casket, which is also incorrect, and bears the portrait of a fool, symbolizing that he is foolish as to think that he is gold and Portia is silver.

Shakespeare's Guide to Living the Good Life

Back in Venice, Shylock's daughter Jessica wants to marry Bassanio's friend Lorenzo, but Shylock forbids it. Jessica elopes with Lorenzo, taking some of Shylock's precious ducats and gemstones in the process. When Shylock learns that she has fled, he appears more distressed by the loss of his ducats and gemstones than the loss of of his own child.

Bassanio secures the loan from Shylock on Antonio's fleshy collateral, travels to Belmont, and correctly chooses the lead casket, which houses a portrait of Portia and a scroll bearing the following verse:

You that choose not by the view
chance as fair and choose as true!
Since this fortune falls to you,
be content and seek no new.
(*The Merchant of Venice*, act 3, scene 2)

Bassanio marries Portia, and his companion, Gratiano, marries Portia's lady-in-waiting, Nerissa, in a double wedding in Belmont. Thereafter, a messenger reports to them that Antonio's ships have been lost at sea, meaning that he will be unable to pay the loan of three thousand ducats, and Shylock is seeking Antonio's pound of flesh.

Bassanio and Gratiano rush back to Venice to save their friend, Bassanio with enough money now from Portia to pay the loan many times over. Portia's cousin, Bellario, a noted doctor of jurisprudence,

Compassion

has been contacted by the Duke of Venice to decide Shylock's case against Antonio. Portia and Bellario agree that Bellario will claim a prior commitment and Portia will appear in Bellario's place, disguised as a young man named Balthazar, to decide the case in Bellario's stead. Portia brings Nerissa with her to Venice, disguised as her male clerk, Stephano.

At court, Shylock is adamant that he is entitled to enforce the letter of the law. Bassanio has offered to pay three times the amount of the loan to save Antonio's life, but Shylock is blinded by his desire for revenge; he scoffs at the money and insists that the duke award him Antonio's pound of flesh. The duke invites Portia (disguised as Balthazar) to decide the merits of the case. She hears the evidence, reviews the loan, and agrees that Shylock is entitled to enforce the bond. Shylock is giddy with malice and bloodlust, but Portia implores him instead to choose mercy. She is giving him enough rope to hang himself, and he has no idea. When Shylock repeatedly rejects Portia's requests to show compassion, she tells Antonio to prepare to face the blade.

Just as Shylock touches the knife to Antonio's skin, Portia reminds Shylock that the bond calls only for flesh, and not blood. Under Venetian law, if Shylock spills any blood while carving out his pound of flesh, he will have violated the terms of the bond, injured another, and therefore will forfeit "his lands and goods."

Shylock immediately becomes willing to take Bassanio's money instead of Antonio's flesh, but Portia holds him to his original position, wherein he rejected the money moments before. Portia

48   **Shakespeare's Guide to Living the Good Life**

reveals to the courtroom that the charade of the bond was a ruse whereby Shylock could legally execute Antonio with impunity. As such, under Venetian law, Shylock must forfeit half his wealth to his intended victim and the other half to the state. Antonio asks the duke to set aside the state's half of the fine and require Shylock to hold the other half in trust for Lorenzo and Jessica, to be given to them upon Shylock's death. Everyone, except possibly Shylock, receives their happy ending.

Mercy and compassion were as important to the Elizabethans as they are to us today. The divisiveness of the modern world may feel unprecedented, but the growing city of London in the 1500s was full of foreign travelers, people of different religions, and a rigid hierarchy based on land ownership, royal connections, and inherited wealth. Then and now, conflict calls out for individuals to show mercy and compassion to one another.

The play is based on an Italian folktale written by Giovanni Fiorentino in the late 1300s as part of a collection of stories called *Il Pecorone*. Based on Shakespeare's odds-on knowledge of Latin, it is likely that he used the original Italian version, rather than a translation, as the source for *The Merchant of Venice*. The audience would have been familiar with the subject, enjoying the themes of shipwreck, puzzles (Portia's caskets), and courtroom drama, as modern audiences do today.

The Merchant of Venice is another early comedy, likely written between 1596 and 1598. As a young playwright and member of the Lord Chamberlain's Men, Shakespeare was working with crowd-pleasing themes that would resonate with his audience; but the more serious tone in this play may be attributable to the death of his only son, Hamnet, who was buried on August 11, 1596. Shakespeare masterfully presents the emotions of rage and frustration at the injustices rife in this play: Portia treated like chattel, Jessica stifled by her father's harsh rules, Shylock insisting on the letter of the law, and Bassanio flummoxed by his lack of funds, to name a few. Shakespeare conveyed them so clearly because he felt those emotions inside his bones, as any of us would, given the unthinkable circumstance of our own cherished child being taken at the age of eleven. Shakespeare's development as a writer and a communicator is clearly visible in *The Merchant of Venice*.

Portia has always been one of my favorite Shakespeare characters. When I first read *The Merchant of Venice* in a high school English class, she was no different to me than Molly Ringwald in *Sixteen Candles* or Mary Stuart Masterson in *Some Kind of Wonderful*. Portia felt the deep pain of her father's passing, yet rather than being comforted in her grief, she was sentenced to be sold off to the highest riddle-solving bidder. And yet, despite her suffering and infuriating circumstances, she is the most compassionate character in this, one of Shakespeare's most popular plays. I began to wonder if it was her oppression that enabled her to show such compassion, imploring everyone in act 4's courtroom scene to choose mercy over self-righteousness. It also wasn't lost on me that Portia was the smartest person in the play, showing that although you might know more than the next person, it does not give you the right to lord it over them.

Portia could have become the helpless victim of her disempowering circumstances, retreating into resentment, lashing out in anger, or devolving into gloomy silence. Instead, she acts from the heart, offering to help Antonio and ultimately convincing Shylock that compassion and benevolence represent the wiser (and happier) paths. Compassion and mercy, whether you are on the giving or receiving end of their gifts, are essential to living the good life.

Elizabethan England was a time of great frustration for women, who were not permitted to attend school or university, were banned from owning property, and were barred from joining trade guilds. They were in essence owned by their fathers and brothers until they married, at which time their ownership was transferred to their husbands. This is one of the reasons why Queen Elizabeth I, who reigned from 1558 to 1603, chose not to marry. Her royal lineage offered her opportunities that were unavailable to most of her female subjects, and as head regent, she refused all offers of marriage, knowing that she'd be giving her power away to a man if she wed. Many of her advisors tried to force her to marry "for the good of the country," but she knew better. Women were expected to be subservient and silent, and there were many who tried to silence Queen Elizabeth I. She outsmarted them every time. This was the political, economic, and societal climate in which Shakespeare, the father of two daughters, birthed his creative works.

Although Shakespeare wrote some of the greatest female characters in history, Elizabethan women were also prohibited from acting on stage. Thus, it was men who brought Shakespeare's women to life in the theater. And what amazing lives these characters enjoyed—Shakespeare gave his heroines an opportunity to claim their power through his written word, and brought a message of female empowerment to his audience in such an entertaining way that the theatergoers didn't know what hit them.

Portia is one of the most thoughtful and adored of all Shakespeare's characters, male or female. She is the wise-beyond-her-years heiress, restrained by a ridiculous clause in her father's will that forces her to marry the suitor who chooses the correct casket from a choice of three, in a solve-a-riddle, "Let's Make a Deal" kind of way. Shakespeare knew exactly how horrible it was for women living in the late 1500s and early 1600s, and he also knew that they had a capacity for mercy and compassion that allowed them to survive (and sometimes thrive) in a world that devalued them.

Some scholars have surmised that Portia was intended to embody Queen Elizabeth I herself, constrained by the societal restrictions of the time, but working behind the scenes to maintain her power. Queen Elizabeth ruled as "the virgin queen" for nearly forty-five years, refusing to allow any of her critics, heads of foreign states, or political adversaries to wrest power from her or draw her into political warfare. In many ways, Shakespeare's Portia did the same, using her intellect, social awareness, and compassion to thwart Shylock's attempted murder of Antonio, which surely would have occurred without her intervention.

Portia chafes under her father's heartless restrictions. The audience holds its breath while the haughty Prince of Morocco inserts the key in the gold casket. We heave a sigh of relief when he reads the words, "all that glisters is not gold." Thereafter, we're on the edge of our seats again as the supercilious Prince of Arragon unlocks the silver casket and leans back, laughing when it reveals the face of a fool. These scenes are interwoven with comedy, but like Queen Elizabeth I, for whom this play may have been performed at Whitehall Palace, the serious nature of the matter is all too real for many women and other marginalized groups in our society. To think that our future, our search for love, our very existence, can be determined without our consent or authority imparts a feeling of imprisonment and injustice.

Compassion

Shakespeare may not have been a woman (rumors abound that he was merely a front for a female ghostwriter), but he was able to convey the sense of powerlessness that society or government often imposes on a marginalized group of people. Again, this is a universal theme that transcends the centuries with examples that appear in our lives every day.

In my legal career, I was often asked for help by clients who wanted, like Shylock, to "exact their pound of flesh." Many potential plaintiffs erroneously believe punishment to be the purpose of the law, and I spent years disavowing clients of the all-too-common misconception that revenge equals justice. Let me assure you that (1) revenge and justice are not the same; and (2) revenge, whether served cold or warm, causes indigestion in both the giver and the receiver. Frequently, people seek redress through the legal system, but those remedies are already set by law, and many of the remedies are not what most plaintiffs want. What they *really* want is to make someone hurt just as much as they did. Some forms of justice, notably the no-holds-barred variety, if sought for the purpose of punishment, are unlikely to bring the desired peace or satisfaction to any of the parties involved. More often than not, this kind of retaliatory "justice" leaves everyone (except the lawyers, of course) broken, exhausted, and feeling hollow inside.

I don't know how many people and organizations I have dissuaded from pursuing revenge wrapped in a flimsy disguise of righteousness, but I believe that I was channeling Portia by reminding them that "earthly power doth then show likest God's when mercy seasons justice." It reminds me of a saying from one of my favorite T-shirts: "If you have to choose between being kind and being right, choose being kind and you will always be right." Shakespeare could have designed that shirt.

If you're wondering how to nurture those feelings of mercy and compassion in yourself, the modern scientists' approach may sound surprisingly similar to that of your favorite spiritual teacher. Meditation, awareness, mindfulness, breathing, and journaling have all been shown to increase well-being and psychological health. Moreover, research shows that compassion is something that we can develop and embody with exercise and practice. A 2017 study found that a lengthy period of training is not required in order to create noticeable increases in our ability to feel compassion. In that study, one group engaged in compassion intervention that consisted of one ninety-minute meeting per week for three weeks. At each meeting, the group discussed suffering and kindness, engaged in role-playing, and wrote letters to themselves about their future from the perspective of a kind and compassionate friend. The control group did not participate in any intervention. At the end of the study, the group that participated in compassion training had significantly higher life satisfaction, self-compassion, and positive outlook, as compared to the group with no intervention.[1]

Compassion

Why does practicing mercy and compassion lead to a sense of well-being? Studies have shown that it activates certain processing systems in the brain that regulate our fight-or-flight response. When a perceived threat is present, the parasympathetic nervous system activates. This enhances our ability to feel safe and secure.[2] And those feelings in turn encourage compassion and mercy. Our brains are able to create new synaptic connections, which is a concept called neuroplasticity, and researchers have noted the changes that occur in the brain after an individual has practiced being more compassionate, both toward themselves and others.[3]

Shakespeare shows us that when we cultivate compassion in ourselves, it radiates outward, affecting everyone who gives, receives, or witnesses it. To wit, Antonio is saved by Portia's demonstration of compassion, and when Portia spares him from supplying a "pound of flesh," rather than taking any restitution for himself, he requests that the duke give his portion of the award to Shylock's daughter, Jessica, and her new husband, Lorenzo.

Jessica has watched her father become bitter and resentful, and with reason—as a Jewish moneylender in Christian-ruled Venice, his rancor is understandable. Shylock, like Portia, suffers a barrage of unfair and harsh circumstances. But unlike Portia, Shylock devolves into anger and contempt. Jessica, raised on that bitterness, chooses not to follow her father's path of hatred for the Christians of Venice. She elopes with

56   Shakespeare's Guide to Living the Good Life

Lorenzo (a Christian), proof that her ability to choose compassion over hatred allows her to find love, aided by Bassanio and his friend, Gratiano. She and Lorenzo are rewarded with the inheritance that Antonio secures for them. Portia and Bassanio enjoy a happy ending, and even Portia's lady-in-waiting, Nerissa, finds love with Gratiano, who was also on the compassion train when he supported the interfaith marriage of Jessica and Lorenzo.

Enactments

The following enactments are your ticket to compassion—they are intended to improve your relationship with compassion and mercy, activate your brain's neuroplasticity, and help you to share those feelings of goodwill. This brings the good life to you and the world at large.

Consciously Recall a Time of Mercy

When you are wanting to cultivate your capacity for compassion, take a few minutes to do this meditation practice. To start, sit in a quiet place and close your eyes. Consciously recall a time when someone showed mercy to you, possibly in a situation when you didn't expect it. Were you traveling? Did you find yourself in unfamiliar circumstances? Were you feeling vulnerable? Remember what the person said or did that demonstrated mercy. How did that make you feel? Did you relax? Did you feel connected to that person? Did their actions seem extraordinary, like receiving a gift? Now remember your response to receiving mercy. What did you do or say? Did the offer of kindness spark a conversation? Think about that experience and contemplate how you might offer mercy in a similar situation in the future.

Make a Commonality List

Is there a person or a group that you feel yourself judging or condemning? Does it create tension in your body and cause you to lose sleep at night? If so, a commonality list may help. To start, make a list of at least ten things that you have in common with the person or members of the group. If you get to ten relatively quickly, keep going until you can't think of any more common traits, conditions, or experiences. If you're not sure what you have in common, do a bit of research to find out more about the person or group. You may find that the similarities become more important than the differences, or that what you initially thought you knew about the person or group is no longer the case. After reviewing the list, notice what emotions are present. Do you feel more compassion? Do you have the ability to offer mercy? Has the negative charge when you think of the person or group diminished? If so, jot down the changes and review them from time to time.

58   Shakespeare's Guide to Living the Good Life

Repeat a Mercy Mantra

If you're having trouble connecting with someone close to you, or you'd like to foster a better relationships with an acquaintance, try this exercise. To start, visualize yourself in a place where you feel safe, loved, and protected. Bring to mind an individual from whom you feel disconnected. If, like Shylock, you are conjuring ways to exact a pound of flesh from a certain person, you may want to choose someone who elicits a milder response from you to start.

Imagine the individual sitting in front of you a few feet away, facing you. Repeat a mantra as you picture them: "May you be well, may you be free from suffering, may you experience happiness." Visualize health and safety for yourself and for the other person. Repeat this enactment with anyone else with whom you feel a negative charge, estrangement, or alienation.

Chapter Four

Persistence
All's Well That Ends Well

In Rossillion, France, the death of physician Gerard de Narbon is followed closely by the death of his patron, Count Rossillion. The count's heir, Bertram, is sent to Paris as a ward of the King of France, and Helen, the deceased physician's daughter who is madly in love with Bertram, is distraught at his departure.

When Bertram arrives in Paris, the King of France is at death's door, suffering from a fistula that scores of surgeons and apothecaries cannot cure. Bertram chafes under the stifling confinement he perceives as a newly arrived courtier to the king; he wants to be in Italy, fighting in the war between Florence and Siena, where the King of France refuses to intervene and encourages young French soldiers seeking battle experience (and an opportunity to sow their wild oats) to join either side of the Tuscan conflict. To Bertram's great dismay, the king determines that the puerile count is too young for the war and must stay at court for another year.

Bertram's older companion, the foppish braggadocio and clotheshorse Parolles, encourages Bertram to defy the king and hone his battle sword on the Tuscan front (in more ways than one; Shakespeare loves a good pun). Although Bertram trusts Parolles, others believe the old popinjay to be a fraud and poltroon. He tells vivid and elaborate tales of his warring escapades, but his supercilious nature belies his adventurous yarns.

The countess's and king's friend, Lafew, invites Helen to Paris, and persuades the king to allow her to apply her healing knowledge to his agonizing ulcer. When she successfully cures the king, he gives her a ring as a token of his appreciation and grants her the choice of any of his young nobles in marriage. She of course chooses Bertram, who peevishly tries to resist the king's decree; not only can he not sow his oats and test his mettle on the Tuscan battlefields, but he also is being forced to marry the lowborn daughter of his father's physician.

The king, freshly cured and flexing his royal power, gives Bertram the choice of marriage or banishment, and Bertram begrudgingly accepts his matrimonial fate. Before the marriage is consummated, however, Bertram runs away to Italy with Parolles and several French soldiers, leaving Helen with a letter that says he shall not be her husband until two conditions are met, both of which he states are inconceivable: (1) she takes his ancestral ring from him (which he claims will never leave his finger); and (2) she shows him a child they conceived together (which he claims to be an impossibility because he will never see her again).

Helen, one of the most adored characters in Shakespeare's oeuvre, is undaunted. She gets to work on what she perceives to be Bertram's "to-do" list for her. She steals away, leaving a note indicating that she is going on a pilgrimage to Saint Jacques le Grand. Instead, she shadows Bertram and makes her way to Tuscany, where her husband in name only is fighting for the Duke of Florence. Soon thereafter, Helen sends anonymous letters to the countess proclaiming that she died of a broken heart while on her pilgrimage, including a verification purportedly from the rector of Saint Jacques. Upon hearing the news that he is a widower, Bertram attempts to woo and marry a noble Florentine virgin, Diana.

As Shakespeare would have it, though, Diana meets Helen, and the two conspire to trick Bertram into assisting Helen with the fanciful "to-do" list—namely, the exchange of rings and physical consummation of the marriage. Diana implores Bertram to give her his ancestral ring in exchange for her virginity, which she promises later that evening if he will visit her chamber after dark. He complies, and it is Helen who lies with Bertram, conceives his child, and gives him the king's ring as a token of her love. Thinking her to be Diana, Bertram is none the wiser.

At the same time, Parolles's insufferable exaggerations of "gallant militarism" have spurred Bertram's friends to pull a prank on him, to prove once and for all that the foppish dandy is a coward and a liar. As Parolles laments to Bertram and his colleagues the loss of a battle drum, the nobles goad him into stealing behind enemy lines to recover it, knowing full well that he will never do so.

Persistence

Parolles takes the bait, and is ambushed when he is hiding out, rehearsing a manufactured tale of bravery to excuse his failure to recover the drum. A few French soldiers are solicited to kidnap and blindfold Parolles, speaking in made-up Italian gibberish, and eventually bring him to Bertram, where a French soldier acting as "interpreter" demands that Parolles divulge his army's secrets to save his life. Parolles sings like a canary, not only giving away all the army's secrets, but disparaging Bertram and his friend Captain Dumaine in the process. The blindfold is removed and Parolles, revealed as a coward, liar, and traitor, is stripped of his courtier status. The city-states of Florence and Siena negotiate a truce, and everyone returns to Rossillion, where the countess and Lafew are entertaining the king.

Still in league with Helen, Diana follows Bertram to Rossillion, and accuses him before the king and his courtiers of violating her honor. Bertram denies it and accuses her of fraud, but she shows the king the ancestral ring that "she" cajoled from him in exchange for "her" virginity. In addition, Bertram wears the ring that the king gave to Helen, and the courtiers surmise, based on Bertram's disdain of Helen, that he was somehow involved in Helen's untimely death. Diana leaves the king with a riddle about the quick rising from the dead, and the court is shocked when a pregnant Helen appears in Rossillion, bearing Bertram's ancestral ring, his child, and his letter that says when those two conditions have been met, he shall be her husband. Bertram, healed by Helen's magic touch, professes his love for her, stating, "If she, my liege, can make me know this clearly, I'll love her dearly, ever, ever dearly."

Stories about characters who persist to reach their goals against impossible odds were as popular in Shakespeare's time as they are today. *All's Well That Ends Well*, which many scholars believe was written sometime in 1598, is a nontraditional comedy based on the tale of Giletta di Narbona from Boccaccio's *The Decameron*. The tale was part of a collection of short stories published in Italy two hundred years before Shakespeare's birth. Although Shakespeare had learned Latin as part of his grammar school education and probably could have read *The Decameron* in its original Italian, the tales had also been translated into French and were circulating around England at least thirty years before Shakespeare tackled the subject. In addition, William Painter translated the book into English in his 1566 collection entitled *The Palace of Pleasure*, which meant that many in the Elizabethan audience were familiar with the story.

Shakespeare, as a playwright honing his writing chops and working to expand the comedic genre in London, added some interesting layers to his characters, particularly Bertram, who is often characterized as unlikeable and unworthy of Helen's affection. Roger, the main character in the original story from

The Decameron, was much kinder to the physician's daughter, and begged off the marriage because he was a confirmed bachelor, not because he thought the physician's daughter was too lowly born for him. In *All's Well That Ends Well*, Shakespeare experiments with the notion of class discrimination and tackles the difficult job of creating a sympathetic male lead whom the audience roots for despite his mistreatment of the female lead. Shakespeare's expanding literary proficiency is undeniable here, portraying Bertram as a horrible judge of character, equally inept in recognizing Helen's virtues as he is in failing to recognize Parolles's vices. We all probably know someone who suffers from Bertram's particular form of social blindness.

To modern audiences, Helen may seem like your typical plucky female heroine, but in the sixteenth century, she was more of an anomaly. An understanding of Elizabethan hierarchies clarifies the nature of Helen's enduring will, because sixteenth-century England was mired in the classism of royalty, nobility, landed gentry, courtiers, a growing merchant class, soldiers, trade and guild workers, and peasants. Despite a female regent in Queen Elizabeth I, most women held a lower societal status than their male counterparts. Shakespeare's audience would have well understood Helen's disadvantaged societal position: she is a woman, a physician's daughter (i.e., working class), an unmarried virgin, and an orphan. She is prohibited from improving her situation, her opinions are dismissed, and her only virtue is her virginity, which society expects her to give to any man who chooses her, and not vice versa. It is with these odds stacked against her that Helen sets a near-impossible goal for herself, then proceeds to achieve it.

When I first read this play, Helen was not the only character who impressed me. I was struck by the persistence of all the female characters, who remain strong and true to themselves in an environment that restricts their value and their voices. I truly admire the eloquence with which Countess Rossillion shares her knowledge and wisdom with her son as he's leaving home to serve the king. Anyone who has sent a child off to kindergarten or college understands her angst. The countess managed to keep it together and give her son a treasure trove of sage advice: "love all, trust a few, do wrong to none"; "keep thy friend under thy own life's key"; and "be checked for silence but never taxed for speech." I wish I could have channeled her wisdom when my daughters left home for school, but I didn't because I was trying too hard not to cry.

Similarly, Diana of Florence meets Helen and upon hearing of Helen's daunting goal, jumps in and offers her assistance. Diana, like Helen, has lost her father and has few prospects, but she has her wits and the will to help a stranger whose plight feels all too familiar. She travels from Florence to Rossillion, France, and appears before the king to support her newfound friend. As a reward for her bravery, the king promises Diana a dowry as well as the choice of a husband from among the king's courtiers. Diana's wit, grit, and persistence, like Helen's, were commended and compensated by the king, and she received a happy ending as well.

It's possible that Shakespeare drew from Queen Elizabeth I when crafting these feminine models of perseverance. Life in Elizabethan England was not easy for the citizens or the monarch: there were food shortages, catastrophic weather events, political turmoil, the bubonic plague, and religious conflicts. That's why Queen Elizabeth I was always on her guard—during her reign, there were at least four elaborate plots to assassinate her and enthrone her Catholic half sister, Mary, Queen of Scots. Elizabeth I embodied the concepts of grit and persistence, both of which probably kept her alive as sovereign during the forty-five-year period that included the publication and performance of most of Shakespeare's plays. Shakespeare channels this grit and persistence in Helen, Diana, and the countess, showing that these characteristics exist in all of us, regardless of social position. Further, the groundlings watching from the cheap seats must have loved the fact that the "commoners" (Helen and Diana) outwitted the landed gentry (Bertram) to secure their own positive outcomes.

Shakespeare did not limit the plucky persistence to his female characters. Bertram's companion, Parolles, the classic and comic poseur, also shows his "don't give up" attitude in this hilarious scene with Helen:

PAROLLES
Little Helen, farewell. If I can remember
thee, I will think of thee at court.

HELEN
Monsieur Parolles, you were born under a
charitable star.

PAROLLES
Under Mars, I.

HELEN
I especially think under Mars.

PAROLLES
Why under Mars?

HELEN
The wars hath so kept you under that you
must needs be born under Mars.

PAROLLES
When he was predominant.

HELEN
When he was retrograde, I think.

PAROLLES
Why think you so?

HELEN
You go so much backward when you fight.
(*All's Well That Ends Well*, act 1, scene 1)

Parolles is witty and fun-loving, and although Helen sees through his thin veneer, Parolles continues to push his war-weary veteran narrative to anyone who will listen. Bertram believes his courtier-companion's tall tales, but Bertram's friends perceive immediately that Parolles is more scaramouch than soldier. After being exposed and stripped of his veteran combatant facade, Parolles continues to fight for himself, using his cleverness and charm to improve his prospects. He soon sets his sights on employment with another nobleman:

PAROLLES
Good Monsieur
Lavatch, give my lord Lafew this letter. I have ere
now, sir, been better known to you, when I have
held familiarity with fresher clothes. But I am
now, sir, muddied in Fortune's mood, and smell
somewhat strong of her strong displeasure.

FOOL
Truly, Fortune's displeasure is but sluttish if it
smell so strongly as thou speak'st of. I will henceforth
eat no fish of Fortune's butt'ring. Prithee,
allow the wind.

PAROLLES
Nay, you need not to stop your nose, sir. I
spake but by a metaphor.

FOOL
Indeed, sir, if your metaphor stink I will stop my
nose, or against any man's metaphor. Prithee, get

70   **Shakespeare's Guide to Living the Good Life**

thee further.

(*All's Well That Ends Well*, act 5, scene 2)

Parolles's continued faith in his own value and his dogged determination to seek a position with Count Lafew are rewarded with a hopeful ending in relative luxury as Lafew's personal attendant. All's well that ends well, as Shakespeare says.

When I was in college, I had the honor of camping out at K-ville, a tent city that sprang up before highly anticipated men's basketball games at Duke University. Living in temporary polyester housing for days leading up to each game was the only way to ensure a seat in the student section of Cameron Indoor Stadium to watch, up close and personal, one of the best basketball programs in the country. Our beloved Blue Devils reached the national championship my freshman year, and by my sophomore year I had the notion that if I could somehow make the cheerleading squad, I would have front-row seats to every home game without having to sleep outside on the cold ground during the two frostiest months of the year. (Winter in central North Carolina is not as balmy as one might think.)

Like Shakespeare's heroine, Helen, several people tried to talk me out of my impossible dream of making the cheer team. After all, I was an introvert with 20-800 vision and the endurance of a giant panda; this was a vigorous program and supercompetitive to boot. Everyone and their sister wanted

Persistence   71

courtside seats for the best college basketball games in the United States. Although I didn't have much going for me on paper, I, like the female characters in *All's Well That Ends Well*, had an objective in mind and the will to make it happen. I swallowed my fears, broke the ice, ignored the odds, sweated buckets, burned the midnight oil, and grew new muscles. I could ride this metaphor train forever, but you get the gist. After the first week of tryouts, I was so sore that walking to class felt like climbing Mount Everest.

During the final week of tryouts, the entire top-ten-ranked basketball team came to watch. (Because who doesn't want another level of stress added to an already daunting situation?) In a panic, I removed my contacts and allowed my natural 20-800 vision to turn the crowd into a blue blur as we performed the final routines. We were told the new team roster would be posted at 6:00 p.m. that Friday. I was a ball of nerves as I exited my Friday afternoon class en route to the student union. My stomach was churning and my heart was sparking in my chest like a live electrical wire. Inside the lobby of the Cambridge Inn Student Union (which, by the way, looks like an Elizabethan wood-paneled venue where Shakespeare's gang might have staged a play), I frantically scanned the list.

My heart sank as I my eyes swept down the list from the top—there were sixteen spots, and I didn't see my name. I continued toward the end and my name was the last one there. I almost didn't believe it—I had made it by the skin of my teeth!

Despite the odds and the naysayers, my persistence had paid off. I'll never forget that feeling. Satisfaction spread throughout my whole body as I celebrated the results of focusing on a goal and doggedly working toward it. As I reflected on my journey, I realized that it was not just that moment of elation, but all of the challenging moments leading up to it that created my experience of the good life.

Many of us can relate to the feeling that our challenges are insurmountable. Regardless of whether you are an Elizabethan with no indoor plumbing or a twenty-first-century working parent with not enough hours in the day, Shakespeare's message is that we have a choice: allow our circumstances to overwhelm us, or break our long-range goals into smaller chunks and move incrementally toward them with faith and fortitude. If we choose grit, we are experiencing a rewarding component of the good life, and if we need a little help reaching our own happy ending, we can look to the characters in *All's Well That Ends Well* to break persistence down into the five Cs: clarity, commitment, creativity, courage, and community.

Enactments

The next time you find yourself facing an obstacle, try incorporating these enactments into your victory strategy. Channel your inner Helen as you take on the challenge!

Celebrate the Little Wins

Breaking down an ambitious goal into smaller goals and rewarding ourselves for incremental successes is a great way to develop persistence, or pluck, as my grandmother used to call it. When we make progress on those smaller steps, it reenergizes us and increases our will to accomplish the goal. I'm a fan of making lists; it's extremely satisfying to cross items off when they've been accomplished. If you have a significant goal in mind, make a list of the small steps leading to that goal, and as you sally forth, mark each completed step with a gold star, smiley face, or a great big red line through it. Celebrating the little wins helps to keep our eye on the prize without becoming overwhelmed, allowing us to get exactly what we want—just like Helen.

Recall Your Resilience

Reflecting on past experiences is a proven method for developing grit and improving our resilience so we can continue moving toward our aspirations. We are hardwired to remember our failures so we don't repeat them, but if we spend too much time focusing on them, it can sap us of motivation to take on a new challenge. When we turn our attention to those occasions where we confronted a problem and successfully managed it, we are reminded of our strengths and accomplishments. Those reminders can inspire us to pursue a new project. For this enactment, recall a time when you were faced with an obstacle that seemed insurmountable. How did you rise to the challenge? As you reflect, be sure to acknowledge and appreciate your own resourcefulness, knowing that you'll be able to tackle the next challenge just as handily. You got this.

Partner Up for Persistence

Another great way to maintain your grit is to remember that in most cases, you do not have to walk a solitary path. Helen did not face her obstacles alone—she enjoyed the camaraderie and support that she received from Countess Rossillion and Diana, which enabled her to reach her goals. And I didn't teach myself cheerleading in college, either—I had lots of help from Maxine and Anne, who graciously helped me with the routines and gave me feedback on my form. And my roommates cheered me on when I wasn't sure whether what I was doing would be worth it in the end. Remember that, whether they're visible or not, behind pretty much all major achievement is a base of support. Family members, teachers, mentors, neighbors, friends—we need each other to survive and thrive. Don't be afraid to ask for help when you need it.

Chapter Five

Communication

Much Ado About Nothing

Don Pedro, Prince of Aragon, and his soldiers arrive in Messina after a successful military conquest against his brother, Don John. Don Pedro and Don John reconcile after the battle and travel together with Don Pedro's soldiers to the home of Messina's governor, Leonato. The jovial governor welcomes Don Pedro and his military retinue to relax, repose, and recharge after the wars. An exceedingly jocular soldier named Benedick spars verbally with Leonato's niece Beatrice, and we learn that these combatants in a "merry war" have a history—one in which, according to Beatrice, Benedick won her heart with "false dice." When she realized the deception, she put him down "lest [she] should prove the mother of fools."

As Benedick and Beatrice continue their war of words, Claudio falls in love with Leonato's daughter, Hero. At a masque that evening, Don Pedro volunteers to woo Hero in Claudio's name, and after a successful encounter, Claudio and Hero make plans to marry in a public celebration. Claudio, Hero, Leonato, and Don Pedro are so thrilled with the impending nuptials that they consort to trick Benedick and Beatrice into falling in love with each other.

The sullen and vanquished Don John is disgusted by the happy celebrations. The night before the wedding, he fools Claudio and Don Pedro into thinking that Hero is unfaithful. He drags them beneath Hero's bedroom window, where Hero's waiting woman, Margaret, kisses Don John's coconspirator, Borachio, in the moonlight. Borachio falsely calls out "Hero" in his ecstasy, and Claudio and Don Pedro believe the worst. They publicly humiliate Hero before the wedding vows are taken and she faints dead away. As the bridal party disperses in shock, Leonato, the officiant friar, and Benedick agree to hide Hero and pretend she's dead until they get to the bottom of the false accusation.

Meanwhile, the matchmaking ruse works on Benedick and Beatrice, who have fallen in love with each other. They finally profess their true feelings, but Beatrice asks Benedick to demonstrate his love by killing Claudio. Benedick agrees to challenge Claudio and defend Hero's honor.

Unaware of the scandalous events, the comedic constable Dogberry and his long-suffering subordinates catch Don John's attendants, Borachio and Conrade, secretly discussing their participation in the crime against Hero. Dogberry extracts a confession from Borachio and Conrade, learning that Don John has paid them one thousand ducats to frame the innocent Hero, thus inciting Claudio to publicly shame her on their wedding day. Borachio's and Conrade's confessions are recorded by the town clerk, who informs them that Hero has died of heartbreak and Don John has fled Messina. Dogberry brings the knaves to Leonato, where they again confess their crimes, which, according to the town clerk, include the murder of Hero.

Claudio is grief-stricken and agrees to submit to any punishment that Leonato devises for him, including death. Leonato demands that Claudio swear before the friar to marry Leonato's never-before-seen niece as retribution for Hero's death. Claudio agrees, and the next day he swears to marry the veiled woman, who lifts her veil to reveal that she is Hero:

And when I lived, I was your other wife,
and when you loved, you were my other husband.
(*Much Ado About Nothing*, act 5, scene 4)

Hero explains that she was dead while her slander lived, but once her slander was made public, she returned to life.

Benedick and Beatrice are asked whether they love each other and initially attempt to deny it, but Claudio presents a love letter to Beatrice written by Benedick and Hero presents a love letter to Benedick written by Beatrice:

BENEDICK
A miracle! Here's our own hands against
our hearts. Come, I will have thee, but by this light
I take thee for pity.

Communication

BEATRICE
I would not deny you, but by this good day, I
yield upon great persuasion, and partly to save your
life, for I was told you were in a consumption.
(*Much Ado About Nothing*, act 5, scene 4)

As Benedick and Beatrice kiss, a messenger arrives to report that Don John has been arrested by armed men and returned to Messina, whereupon Benedick promises Don Pedro that he will devise "brave punishments" for the villain.

Clear communication is one of the most important aspects of our human existence. More than four hundred years ago, Shakespeare wrote this smart and scampish comedy about that very theme, and it may have had its origins in his relationship with one of his acting colleagues, Will Kemp. *Much Ado About Nothing* was entered in the Stationers' Register on August 23, 1600, and published in the first (and only) quarto that same year. The title page of the quarto states that the play "hath beene sundrie times publikely acted by the Right Honourable, the Lord Chamberlaine his servants." There are several notations that the over-the-top and wacky character Dogberry was played by Elizabethan actor and comedian Will Kemp.

However, by the time the play had been registered for publication, Will Kemp had resigned from the Lord Chamberlain's Men. Some believe that Kemp's penchant for overacting may have caused tension with Shakespeare, leading Kemp to seek his jig-loving fortunes elsewhere, and there is ample evidence to support this theory. Kemp left the Lord Chamberlain's Men to perform a traveling one-man morris-dancing show across England, France, and eventually Rome. That Kemp would have chosen to leave a lucrative opportunity in a profitable acting troupe just coming into its own leads many historians to believe that Kemp felt his talents were more suited to a solo career than the shared accolades of an acting company. Kemp had quite a following in the late 1590s, and his acrobatic jigs, which often followed the performance of a stage play, gave him a dash of celebrity that may have gone to his head, causing him to go off-script with increasingly over-the-top and outrageous gags on stage.

Shakespeare's plays are full of disdain for these types of mawkish and histrionic portrayals: "O, it offends me to the soul to hear a robustious, periwig-pated fellow tear a passion to tatters, to very rags, to split the ears of the groundlings," and "O, there be players I have seen play . . . that have so strutted and bellowed that I have thought some of nature's journeymen had made men and not made them well, they imitated humanity so abominably" (*Hamlet*, act 3, scene 2). I think it's likely that Shakespeare had communication and relationships

Communication 81

on the brain when he sat down to pen *Much Ado About Nothing* sometime in 1598.

Relationships don't exist without communication, and the relationship between Hero and Claudio is one the Elizabethans knew well from the ancient Greek tragedies. However, it is the complicated relationship between Beatrice and Benedick that has its more recent origins in a 1588 translation of Baldesar Castiglione's *The Book of the Courtier.* This Italian classic includes an interesting note that when the men and women gather for celebration, in addition to the pleasant pastimes of music and dancing, "sometimes ingenious games were devised at the choice of one or another, in which under various disguises the company disclosed their thoughts figuratively to whom they liked best . . . or biting retorts [were] passed back and forth."[1] These "ingenious games" feature prominently in *Much Ado About Nothing.*

The first memorable performance of this play for me was the 1993 movie directed by Kenneth Branagh and featuring an all-star cast. Branagh played Benedick to his then-wife Emma Thompson's Beatrice, with Denzel Washington as the regal Don Pedro, Kate Beckinsdale as the ingenue Hero, Beetlejuice-esque Michael Keaton as Dogberry, and in a surprising twist, Keanu Reeves as the dark and brooding Don John.

The play begins with the victorious soldiers Don Pedro, Benedick, and Claudio returning from battle, happy to have discarded their armor and aggression for rest and revelry.

Although the vanquished Don John is with them, he is not in the mood to celebrate, and Leonato and the villagers are tasked with helping the soldiers transition back to a more normal postwar existence, unsure if the military men will appreciate their bucolic ways.

It is obvious from the beginning of the play that no one is telling the truth about how they really feel. In 1993, the movie spoke directly to the way I felt at that time in my life: it didn't feel safe to disclose my authentic self, so I hid my true feelings about almost everything—the books I read, my love of Shakespeare, the foods I ate, the fact that I didn't really like to socialize, my thoughts on politics, and my view of the world. Like the characters over the course of the play, I was challenged to become vulnerable and communicate my truth, despite feeling uncomfortable. (I'm still working on that.) The tied-up-with-a-bow ending of *Much Ado About Nothing* comes to fruition only when the characters feel secure in communicating their heartfelt truths. Shakespeare's message is simple: living the good life includes communicating clearly, with integrity, from the heart.

The fact that the main male characters in the play are soldiers has always seemed significant to me. As the story progresses, the soldiers remove their physical armor, yet they find it more difficult to remove the metaphorical armor that protects their truths. I believe this is one of Shakespeare's most popular plays because it demonstrates the many ways in which we cover our feelings to protect ourselves from being hurt. Shakespeare shows us through humor and mishap that the only way to *truly* develop a relationship with another is by throwing off all our armor to reveal our authentic selves.

Like the characters in *Much Ado About Nothing*, we all wear some kind of shield. Whether it consists of facial expression, body language, tone of voice, clothing, hairstyle, adornment, or the company we keep, we are all presenting a stylized mask to the world, hoping that no one will peer behind it. Why? An unprotected soldier will not last long on the battlefield. Benedick comically volunteers to go to the ends of the earth rather than tell Beatrice the truth:

BENEDICK
Will your Grace command me any service
to the world's end? I will go on the slightest errand
now to the Antipodes that you can devise to send
me on. I will fetch you a toothpicker now from the
furthest inch of Asia, bring you the length of Prester
John's foot, fetch you a hair off the great Cham's
beard, do you any embassage to the Pygmies, rather
than hold three words' conference with this harpy.
(*Much Ado About Nothing*, act 2, scene 1)

When Don Pedro asks Beatrice why she is so tough on Benedick, she gives a hint as to the reason she is using her sharp words as a shield:

DON PEDRO
Come, lady, come, you have lost
the heart of Signior Benedick.

BEATRICE
Indeed, my lord, he lent it me awhile, and I
gave him use for it, a double heart for his single
one. Marry, once before he won it of me with false
dice. Therefore your Grace may well say I have lost
it.

(*Much Ado About Nothing*, act 2, scene 1)

Beatrice trusts Don Pedro enough to hint that her heart has
been broken by Benedick, and she vows not to allow that to happen again. Similarly, Claudio wants to speak to Hero, but when
his superior officer, Don Pedro, suggests that he should intercede,
the younger officer acquiesces, rather than offend his boss.

Don John, who appears to have reconciled with his brother
after their battle, wears the heaviest armor. He pretends to
enjoy the festivities at Leonato's home, but when he sees the
opportunity to torment his brother and take down Claudio,
Hero, and Leonato in the process, he jumps at the chance. Don
John reveals his true feelings about his brother to Borachio
only in private: "I am sick in displeasure to him, and whatsoever comes athwart his affection ranges evenly with mine."

Shakespeare cautions us that communicating our truths is
not always easy. Hero alone is the character who is honest with
her feelings from the outset, and she is the one who is most

Communication 85

maligned, an innocent and unwitting victim of a cruel plot. This is a clarion call for all of us: speaking our truths and communicating our authentic beliefs may result in temporary pain or sadness, but it will work out in the end.

This is also true for the treacherous Don John, who, rather than admitting his falsehoods and taking responsibility for his lies, flees Messina in the dark of night, leaving his attendants Borachio and Conrade to take the blame. Similarly, Beatrice and Benedick's reunion is almost derailed when Benedick is on the verge of proclaiming his love for Beatrice but instead asks, "Do you not love me?" He doesn't want to be the first one to admit his affection. This puts Beatrice on notice that he is afraid to communicate his true feelings, which raises her guard, and she responds, "Why no, no more than reason." They are about to follow each other into the rabbit hole of finger-pointing and denial until their friends find love letters in which each has confessed their devotion to the other. When they are caught with the proof of their true feelings on paper, they finally let down their guards and admit the truth:

BENEDICK
In brief, since I
do purpose to marry, I will think nothing to any
purpose that the world can say against it, and
therefore never flout at me for what I have said
against it.

(*Much Ado About Nothing*, act 5, scene 4)

I have been a card-carrying member of the nerd herd since I was a young child. I loved reading books, learning about plants and animals, watching science fiction movies, and spending time alone. The fact that I'm telling you this right now is thanks to what I've learned from Shakespeare about communicating my truth. There is no way in heck I would have admitted my favorite things to most people I met during my childhood and teenage years. Instead, if people asked what I was into, I would deflect and answer as a nondescript member of my family—we waterskied, rode dirt bikes, played softball with the neighborhood kids, and oh, by the way, my dad drove a Corvette. It was easier to pretend I was cool than to experience the waves of pity I got from someone when I told them the truth about my nerdiness.

It wasn't until I entered college and began sharing stories with my roommates that I realized there were lots of people in the world who loved the same things I did. It turns out that a whole group of them took Professor Porter's pre-1600 Shakespeare class with me, and the relief I felt when I was able to share my authentic self with them was like removing a hundred-pound vest I didn't know I was wearing. I wondered how many other people from my childhood I could have connected with if I had only been brave enough to communicate my truth without trying to cover it up by pretending to be "normal."

Communication   87

British neurologist and brain researcher Oliver Sacks famously said, "We speak not only to tell people what we think, but to tell ourselves what we think. Speech is a part of thought." He must have been a fan of *Much Ado About Nothing*, because he perfectly describes the relationship between Benedick and Beatrice: their witty banter not only serves the purpose of learning where the other stands, but also helps to clarify their own feelings about each other.

According to the ancient Greek philosophers, authentic communication requires self-knowledge, benevolence, and a standard of ethical behavior. One must be "sincere, innocent, original, genuine, and unaffected," and transparency is key.[2] Of course, there wouldn't be a play to enjoy if the characters were all transparent with their feelings and opinions, but it's much more pleasurable to enjoy a performance that shows us the pitfalls of inauthentic communication than to experience it ourselves.

If we're not sure whether someone is telling the truth or being authentic, modern science gives us a wonderful tool: kinesics. This is the study of interpreting body language (or nonverbal communication), and it has many uses, from the courtroom to the family room.

An oft-cited statistic about communication states that 55 percent of meaning is transmitted through body language, 38 percent is transmitted through tone of voice, and 7 percent is transmitted through spoken word. This theory was developed

88   **Shakespeare's Guide to Living the Good Life**

by Albert Mehrabian, a psychology professor at UCLA, who published his findings in his 1971 book *Silent Messages*. While there may not be a consensus on the actual percentage break-down, studies have indeed shown that our body language and tone of voice communicate much more than the words being said. Some scientists believe that this occurs because humans initially communicated through physical gestures, which were processed in certain areas of the brain—areas that continue to be activated by the integrated system of communication we use today.[3] It's a relief to know that talking with our hands (and facial expressions) isn't due to a lack of vocabulary, it's simply a result of our evolutionary biology.

This is why wearing virtual armor may not work as well as we believe. Our body knows what we're really thinking and feeling, and the more energy we spend trying to cover that up, the less energy we have for meaningful communication. Alternatively, if we've mastered the art of walling off our true feelings, we may have lost our connection to our own authenticity, which makes it difficult to communicate effectively or develop meaningful relationships.

Shakespeare shows us the folly of inauthentic expression—it is rampant at the beginning of *Much Ado About Nothing*. All of the lying, pretending, stifling, repressing, and camouflaging is exhausting for everyone in the play, and it's just as exhausting in our own lives. Shakespeare gave his characters the courage not only to face their truths, but to communicate them to others. I'm sure we all know plenty of people who, like Beatrice and Benedick, would rather walk barefoot on hot coals than confide a deeply felt emotion to someone else. However, if we want to live the good life, it's up to us to communicate our truths clearly, to ourselves and to the world.

Enactments

These simple and entertaining enactments demonstrate just how complex communication can really be—and they're fun to do with friends!

Act It Out

We are communicating something all the time, whether through the words we say, the feelings we convey, the movement of our bodies, or our energy levels at any given time. The actors on Shakespeare's stage were well known to have used their bodies acrobatically in order to entertain as well as convey a message to the audience. This is a fun kinetic enactment that really helps get in touch with the ways that we can share information with each other.

To start, find at least one friend or family member to play with (as in the theater, the more people who are involved, the more fun this enactment is). If you have only two people total, choose one and tie a bandana or scarf around that person's mouth to cover it completely. The aim is to make sure they cannot use words to communicate. Have the person with the bandana choose a scene from their favorite show or movie and act it out without using any words. The person without the bandana has to guess what they're saying and where the scene comes from. Continue until everyone has had a turn to act out a scene. When you're finished (if you can stop laughing long enough), share the ways in which people were able to communicate that got the message across. Was it their expressive eyes? The ability to raise one or more eyebrows? Hand movements? Stamping or tapping of feet? What did you learn about the ways we communicate with each other without saying a word?

A Score of Lively Interrogatives

Did you notice that the title of this enactment is in iambic pentameter? For me, the good life involves having fun and playing with words, which is what this chapter is all about. A score of lively interrogatives is also known as "twenty questions," "animal, vegetable, mineral," or "person, place, thing." It's a parlor game that's a fun way to practice communication skills and boost creativity.

To start, find a friend or family member—this game requires at least two people, and it is fun to play as a duo, or with a larger group. Choose a person to be "it," which means that they think of a "something" that they keep secret (a celebrity, an animal, a place, or, if you're enjoying the Shakespeare theme, a character in a play). The others in the room are allowed to submit a score of lively interrogatives (aka twenty questions) to figure out what the person designated as "it" has chosen. The questions can only be answered with a "yes" or "no." For example, a famous question from a radio program in the 1940s is: "Is it bigger than a breadbox?" The more imaginative the questions are, the more likely the questioners will guess the answer before they reach twenty questions. As you play, have someone keep track of the questions to make sure you stop at twenty, and see what creative and original ways of communicating and asking questions help you find the answer you're looking for. Continue until each person has an opportunity to be "it," and when you're finished, compare questions and share which answers were the hardest and easiest to deduce.

Chapter Six

Communing with Nature

As You Like It

Orlando, the youngest son of deceased Sir Rowland de Bois, chafes under his oldest brother Oliver's cruel treatment. The siblings are subjects of Duke Frederick, who usurped the throne of his older brother, Duke Senior, and banished him to live in the Forest of Arden. Frederick's daughter Celia was raised with her cousin Rosalind, daughter of the exiled Senior. Because Celia and Rosalind were so close, Frederick agreed not to banish Rosalind with Duke Senior, and she lives in the court with her cousin, estranged from her father.

Oliver de Bois is jealous of his "gentle, strong, and valiant" younger brother, Orlando, and contrives to have him killed in a wrestling match against Oliver's champion wrestler, Charles. However, Orlando bests Charles in the public match, and Rosalind falls in love with the handsome victor. Undeterred, Oliver plots to kill

Orlando in his sleep. But Orlando learns of the planned attack, and he and his senescent attendant, Adam, escape to the forest.

Thereafter, Frederick begins to see Rosalind as a threat, and gives her one day to leave the court or she will be killed. She and Celia gather up their money and run away into the forest together, Rosalind disguised as a youth named Ganymede and Celia assuming the role of Ganymede's sister, Aliena. Their court fool, Touchstone, is appalled by Frederick's behavior, and agrees to travel with them to the Forest of Arden, where they meet a shepherd and purchase a cottage, flock, and pasture to make their new home in the country.

Also arriving in the Forest of Arden, Orlando and Adam are welcomed by Senior and his merry band of exiles, including the brooding and melancholy Jaques. Touchstone befriends Jaques in the woods, and the two avocational philosophers trade their observations about the world. Exploring the woods, Celia discovers love poems to Rosalind posted on the trees, and they learn that the author is none other than Orlando. When they happen upon each other in a copse of trees, Orlando doesn't recognize Rosalind disguised as Ganymede. He confesses his love for Rosalind, who (as Ganymede) offers to cure Orlando of his affliction: if Orlando will pretend that Ganymede is Rosalind and woo Ganymede as Rosalind, Orlando will be healed. Desperate to cure his lovesick heart, Orlando agrees.

Touchstone meets and woos the simple and honest goatherd, Audrey, and prepares for a hasty wedding, but Jaques convinces him to delay it. A local shepherd, Silvius, pines for a neighbor

94   **Shakespeare's Guide to Living the Good Life**

shepherdess, Phoebe, who has fallen in love with Ganymede. The cruel Phoebe writes a love letter to Ganymede and asks her lovesick suitor, Silvius, to deliver it. Ganymede takes pity on Silvius and tries to convince Phoebe to reconsider Silvius as a potential partner.

Orlando's older brother, Oliver, arrives in the forest, surprising Ganymede and Aliena with news that Duke Frederick has ordered him to find and kill Orlando. Instead, Orlando finds Oliver under attack by a lioness, and saves his older brother. The lioness tears the flesh from Orlando's arm, and the brothers manage to limp to old Duke Senior's cave for Orlando to be treated. The ordeal reunites the brothers, and Oliver repents with great remorse and sincerity. Orlando sends Oliver to Ganymede to explain why he missed the daily wooing. Upon hearing the news, Ganymede faints and Aliena falls in love with Oliver.

Aliena and Oliver plan to be married, and Orlando confesses to Ganymede that he is happy that his reformed brother has found love, but the news deepens the agonizing absence of Rosalind from his life. Ganymede promises that Rosalind will appear and marry Orlando the following day. Ganymede extracts Phoebe's promise to marry Silvius the following day as well. Touchstone and Audrey agree to join in the next day's festivities as the third couple to be wed.

In the last scene, Ganymede and Aliena greet the wedding parties and then disappear, only to return as Rosalind and Celia. Rosalind is reconciled with her banished father, old Duke Senior, who performs the wedding ceremony; Oliver learns that his betrothed is not a shepherdess but rather Celia, the daughter of Duke Frederick;

Communing with Nature   95

Phoebe agrees to marry Silvius (because Ganymede exists no more); Audrey is excited to marry Touchstone and become a "woman of the world"; and Orlando is thrilled that his darling Rosalind is prepared to be his bride.

The goddess of marriage, Hymen, descends on the wedding party and blesses the four marriages. In the final deus ex machina, Oliver and Orlando's middle brother, who had been away at school, arrives in the wood with news that Duke Frederick met a religious man who convinced him to give up his crown and convert to a religious life, restoring Duke Senior to his throne and returning all the lands and property to those who were banished with him. Jaques, hearing of the miraculous conversion, embarks on a quest to find Frederick and learn from him. Rosalind delivers the epilogue, entertaining the audience with a wink and nod about gender, saying:

> If I were a woman, I
> would kiss as many of you as had beards that
> pleased me, complexions that liked me, and breaths
> that I defied not. And I am sure as many as have
> good beards, or good faces, or sweet breaths will for
> my kind offer, when I make curtsy, bid me farewell.
> (*As You Like It*, epilogue)

Shakespeare's Guide to Living the Good Life

I can imagine how green and natural Shakespeare's world must have been, especially in Stratford-upon-Avon. The Globe, perched near the banks of the River Thames, was also a beautiful specimen of natural Tudor architecture, with its partially thatched roof and O-shaped walls. Many scholars believe that *As You Like It* was one of the first plays performed in the new Globe Theatre in 1599. The jocular banter between the characters showcases Shakespeare's playfulness with puns and the comedic nature of human beings' behaviors when forced out of their comfort zones. Shakespeare's beloved character Jaques serves as the melancholy commentator, and although his actions do not propel the plot, he serves the same role as the chorus in ancient Greek comedy, drawing the audience into the action with his wry perspective on the wacky happenstances in the Forest of Arden.

Another favorite character, Touchstone, marks a momentous change in Shakespeare's writings following the departure of Will Kemp—Shakespeare no longer writes the "clown" as a dancing, drooling buffoon whose physicality is front and center, because there is a new fool in town: the Lord Chamberlain's Men's newest actor, Robert Armin. Shakespeare's earlier comedies utilize the dramatic role of the "clowne" in a way that was familiar to the Elizabethan audience: Dogberry, Nick Bottom, Launcelot Gobbo, Dromio, etc., are goofy and effusive, using their bodies in aid of the story.

Communing with Nature

The addition of Robert Armin to the company at the same time the new Globe Theatre was erected on the south side of the Thames opened the door to a new kind of fool, one that was articulate, thoughtful, philosophical, and who sang rather than danced. Robert Armin was a ballad writer and skilled singer, an intellectual who had apprenticed as a goldsmith before joining the theater world. He understood his place in the company, and he allowed Shakespeare to add music and even wittier wordplay to the character of the fool. *As You Like It* is a wonderful example of Shakespeare's adaptability, showing that he continued to remain fluid as he faced the changing demands of his craft and his company.

Like the Athenian characters in *A Midsummer Night's Dream,* the French lords and ladies of *As You Like It* throw off the restrictive societal cuffs of the city and flee to the beauty of the forest, some voluntarily and others at sword point. In both cases, however, the change in setting allows them to release the chains that held them to a standard of conduct they may not have otherwise chosen. Nature has that effect on us. The characters' adventures in the forest serve as a guide for us to do the same, releasing limits (known and unknown) as we commune with nature and receive the magic and messages it has for us.

I was aware of Jaques's famous "seven ages of man" speech long before I read or watched a performance of *As You Like It*. The key phrase in that soliloquy—"all the world's a stage"—is a powerful statement that has always resonated with me not only because I believe it to be true, but because it relieved the pressure to achieve that I've felt since I was a young girl. If the world is a stage and we are simply actors on it, then I will always have another performance, another opportunity to change something about myself, or another chance to modify a behavior that feels phony. The same goes for people I encounter—if they frighten, anger, irritate, worry, or sadden me, when I tell myself that they also are playing a role on this world's stage, it gives me compassion to see their actions in a light that softens their impact on me.

The best part about *As You Like It*, however, is the fact that there are several groups of people living a happy and idyllic life in nature, far away from the ridiculous and overbearing rules of society. Yes, I wanted to be Portia from *The Merchant of Venice*, but I also wanted to live in the mythical Forest of Arden, reading the "books in running brooks" and listening to the "sermons in stones." I still do; communing with nature is one of the most important ingredients for living the good life.

As You Like It is best known for its characters, who have been described over the centuries as "brilliant conversationalists." *As You Like It* has provided more one-liners and memorable phrases than any other of Shakespeare's works, including "too much of a good thing," "neither rhyme nor reason," flattery "laid on with a trowel," "a motley fool," "forever and a day," "falser than vows made in wine," "the wise man knows himself to be a fool," "my pride fell with my fortunes," "we

Communing with Nature

have seen better days," "it is but so-so" and time "stands still." The witty repartee among the characters and the contrasting personalities of the fun-loving fool Touchstone and the pensive man-of-the-world Jaques infuse the play with a contemporary flavor that continues to delight. The characters' inspiring conversations arise from their connection to nature, an ever-present source of creative beauty and ideation, then and now.

In *As You Like It*, Shakespeare explores the effects of playfulness, freedom, and egalitarianism on humans who have been forced to behave in ways that may have felt unnatural or unduly competitive at court. In this play's fictional forest, anything is possible. Despite being a thick wood with caves to dwell in, it also boasts pastureland, brooks, rivers, sheep, goats, and lions, none of which are typically found in an old-growth forest. In Shakespeare's imagination, neither a forest nor a person is bound by conventional restrictions.

The coronavirus pandemic offered many the opportunity to leave old paradigms and reconnect with nature, similar to the characters in *As You Like It*. Those who were working in offices Monday through Friday, wearing suits and following protocol, were now wearing whatever was clean, planning meals with family input, playing games, and engaging in meaningful conversations. Dogs all over the world were ecstatic—the usual hurried morning walk magically transformed into multiple leisurely strolls throughout the day. For some, the pandemic provided a time-out that refreshed us for a return to the office,

Shakespeare's Guide to Living the Good Life

like the characters in the forest who eventually returned to court. For others, it led to a completely new life path. In either case, the opportunity to connect with the natural world provides a shift in perspective that makes us more empathetic, caring, and cognizant of the suffering of our brothers and sisters.

Duke Senior, who is cast as a bit of a Robin Hood character, and his fellowship of woodland followers enjoy the freedom of living in the magical Forest of Arden, singing songs, hunting for their meals, sleeping in caves, bathing in lakes and rivers, and communing in consort with the rhythms of Mother Nature:

And this our life, exempt from public haunt,
finds tongues in trees, books in the running brooks,
sermons in stones, and good in everything.
(*As You Like It*, act 2, scene 1)

Far away from the "painted pomp" and "envious court," the foresters have found a freedom and peaceful community that eluded them within the restrictive confines of courtly life. In some ways, life in the timberland may seem more physically demanding, but that is offset by the feeling of camaraderie and the beauty of nature, which offers daily miracles to those who are open to experiencing them.

We were offered the same opportunity during the pandemic: instead of sitting in cars, trains, or airplanes as we

Communing with Nature

commuted to work, many of us spent time outdoors. We rediscovered the rhythms of nature, such as sunrise, sunset, planets and evening stars, and the movement of birds and animals who had been living right under our noses for decades. Studies have shown that the pandemic brought about a resurgence of interest in the interconnectedness of public health, climate change, biodiversity, land use, sustainable agriculture, and renewable sources of energy.[1] It's as if we were unaware of these connections until we had the freedom and time to pause, step back, and observe our place in nature.

Here's a little story about the transformative effects of nature. One Saturday morning not too long ago, my partner and I both woke up early, before sunrise. Despite the beautiful weather, neither of us was feeling right—we both felt restless, uncomfortable, and even though it was the weekend and we could do whatever we wanted, we didn't really feel like doing anything. It was that quintessential funk that comes over every human being now and again. As we sat in the living room feeling lethargic and listless, my partner said, "Why don't we go to the beach?"

Funny how those few simple words perked us up immediately. We put on our swimsuits, packed our towels, threw the dog in the truck, and headed out. Still a bit quiescent, we didn't really talk during the ride. However, the moment we put our feet in the white sand, we were transformed. The sunlight sparkled on the blue water, pelicans were gliding a few feet above the ocean in groups of four and five, a pleasant breeze floated over us to cool the morning heat, and puffy clouds, illuminated pink, purple, and orange by the rising sun, painted a picture so beautiful that it brought tears to our eyes. We ran headlong into the water, feeling renewed. We splashed in the waves, rode them to the shore, and swam back to do it over and over again all morning long. A day that had begun a bit melancholy had been alchemized by the beauty of nature into a glorious beginning to the weekend. This is the power of communing with nature, and one of my favorite parts of living the good life.

The change in environment and pace led us to reconsider our priorities. The results of this introspection—that killing ourselves at work while ignoring our family, friends, neighbors, and furry roommates, is not only unsustainable, but detrimental to our well-being—is a revelation supported by modern science. The Microsoft 2022 Work Trend Index studied more than 31,000 workers in 31 nations and found that the pandemic "reshaped our priorities, identities, and worldview, drawing a bright line between what's important—health, family, time, purpose—and what's not." To wit, 47 percent of those studied stated that they are more likely to put family and personal life over work, and 53 percent of those studied stated that they are now more likely to prioritize health and well-being over work. If we hadn't been temporarily forced to slow

Communing with Nature   103

down and live a more natural existence, we might not have experienced those epiphanies.[2]

Work can provide financial stability and a sense of purpose, but those benefits are diminished when work supplants home, family, health, or well-being. Balance is the key, and nature operates harmoniously, maintaining a perfect balance in its cycles of ebb and flow, phases of the moon, seasons of the year, and so on.

Jaques's famous soliloquy about the seven ages of man—infant, student, lover, soldier, justice, old man, second child—offers another take on the cycle and progression of life. In the modern world, we've been stuck in soldier mode for way too long and it has disrupted the natural cycle of our lives. Fortunately, Mother Nature is always available to help us regain our balance.

Scientific studies have shown that spending time in nature, as little as twenty minutes per day, improves our health in two primary ways—by restoring our capacity to focus and by reducing stress.[3] Taking a walk in the park, swimming, or simply sitting under a tree enables us to overcome the fatigue of modern life and restore our capacity to direct our attention.[4] In one study, viewing nature on a video also reduced stress, as determined by reduced heart rate, less muscle tension, and lower blood pressure.[5]

The characters in *As You Like It* experience similar transformations. Rather than worrying about which brother inherits what lands, who is wrestling whom for status (or retribution), what courtiers are conniving to earn a place of favor with the elite classes, or who throws the biggest and most lavish parties at court, the merry band of new shepherds are entertaining each other with songs about the greenwood tree, sharing their meals and humble caves with visitors, caring for the elderly, pursuing their love interests, and writing poetry.

When Orlando arrives with his aging attendant, Adam, he expects the inhabitants of the forest to be savages and brandishes his sword, ready to protect his weak companion. Instead, he is offered hospitality as a friend. Duke Senior promises that not one of his merry band will eat until Adam has been fed and cared for. Living in the forest, Duke Senior and his fellowship have learned that nature's bounty is always available, and is intended to be shared. The ideas of greedy competition, survival of the fittest, and scarcity were not necessary in the forest. Those notions were replaced with heartfelt compassion, as Duke Senior earnestly wants to help Orlando, saying:

Give me your hand,
and let me all your fortunes understand.
(*As You Like It*, act 2, scene 7)

I feel a kinship to the characters in *As You Like It*, as my own journey has been one of moving from the restrictions of a career in the practice of law to a more freeing pursuit of creativity and thoughtfulness through writing. There certainly

Communing with Nature

is a hierarchy in the practice of law and, unfortunately, also a patriarchy that requires certain behaviors in order to succeed. My own metaphorical Forest of Arden became available during the pandemic, when I no longer traveled for work or attended meetings in person, and instead engaged in more meaningful activities such as writing, walking in nature, living more in tune with my environment, and spending time with family.

The conclusion of *As You Like It* provides a reunion and reconciliation of brothers Frederick and Senior as well as Oliver and Orlando. Fathers and daughters are also reunited, as Celia reconciles with Frederick and Rosalind reveals herself to Senior. In addition, four marriage ceremonies are shared, lands are restored to their rightful owners, and our melancholy commentator, Jaques, is off on a new adventure to discover the mysteries of the world. Shakespeare offers us the chance for a similar happy ending if we take the time to commune with nature, release the limitations imposed on us by society, and explore the unknown.

Enactments

The healing power of nature is available to everyone, and it doesn't take long for its effects to transform body and soul. This awesome and incredible gift isn't limited to landmark nature spaces, either. Nature is literally right outside your door, no matter where you live. Doing something as simple as noticing the arrival of birdsong and daffodils in the spring, the thrum of cicadas and frogs in summer, or the change in the air as fall arrives can bring you back into your body and back in connection with all living beings around you. Taking the time to appreciate the many forms of life around you can be life-changing.

Hug a Tree

I can personally attest to the benefits of hugging a tree, and it's fun to experiment with the feelings that are evoked from hugging certain trees. Hugging a tree, especially an old, sturdy oak or pine, makes me cry almost every time. In fact, when I feel like my emotions are bottled up, I often walk the forest trails, give my favorite trees a hug, and have a cathartic cry. I always feel better when I do. Maybe you have fond memories of lazy days swinging from a tire suspended from a sycamore tree in your grandparents' yard. Hugging a sycamore might feel different than hugging a maple or walnut tree. Experiment with different trees and write down your experiences. Here's how to get started.

Scope out a tree with a wide trunk, one that looks substantial and has been around for many years. It could be one that you've eyed in a park, or one that you pass on your way to work. If you have a favorite walking trail, pick a tree that calls out to you. When you encounter the tree you've chosen, offer a silent prayer of gratitude for the shade, oxygen, beauty, and protection that the tree has provided to every person, insect,

Communing with Nature 107

and animal who passes by. Wrap your arms around the trunk of the tree and breathe deeply. (If you feel uncomfortable giving the tree a hug, simply lean against it or place one or two hands on the trunk, continuing to breathe deeply.) Take a moment to listen to your heartbeat. As you continue to breathe slowly, tune into the sounds that you hear—birds chirping, insects buzzing, leaves rustling, squirrels chattering. Do you feel connected to everything around you? Notice what thoughts, emotions, and memories arise that seem unrelated to your surroundings. Do you feel the urge to cry? If so, let it out. As Shakespeare tells us, there are "tongues in trees," and they may be inviting you to share in a conversation with nature. Observing nature provides us the opportunity to learn more about ourselves.

Walk or Ride Your Bike

If you live in the United States, you very likely drive everywhere for your daily activities—school, work, grocery store, errands, restaurants, coffee shops, parks, and friends' homes. I often drive to a state park near our home to walk our dog on the nature trails that encircle the park. Frankly, I don't pay much attention to the drive until I get to the parking lot and get out of the car. One afternoon, I realized that I hadn't ridden my bike in a long time, and I decided to ride to the park for some exercise. It was like traveling to a completely different place! I noticed tortoises, woodpeckers feeding their young, an osprey with a fish in its talons, and the enchanting scent of honeysuckle. I hadn't seen the honeysuckle blooming, though I daily drove the same road I was now biking. Society often encourages us to be in a hurry so we can accomplish more in a shorter time. Sometimes the hurried lifestyle causes us to miss what's important, limiting our experiences. This enactment asks you to release those limitations by slowing down and noticing nature that you are usually moving too fast to perceive.

Pick a route near your home that you usually drive. It could be the streets in your neighborhood, recreation fields where your children play sports, the grounds surrounding your local library, or a nearby campground. Walk or ride your bike along the same route that you typically drive. Give yourself plenty of time to stop along the route and notice things that you have never seen before. Where is your attention drawn? Are there sights that you observe that you never noticed? Are there sounds that you've never heard on this route? Does the route seem different now that you are taking the time to soak it in? Do you encounter any neighbors or have conversations that you wouldn't have had in the car? How does that feel? Write what you observe, including sights, sounds, smells, and the textures of things that you would not have the opportunity to experience while driving past them. The next time you drive that route, do you find yourself noticing the things that you discovered on your slower-paced adventure? Think about any places where your drive could be replaced with a walk or a bike ride. Slowing down can be an adventure.

Communing with Nature

Chapter Seven

Thinking for Yourself

Julius Caesar

Julius Caesar begins with tribunes (elected representatives of the Roman common classes) Marcellus and Flavius lamenting Caesar's accumulation of power and chastising their lower-born constituents (including a carpenter and cobbler) for celebrating Caesar's return to Rome after a series of successful military campaigns. The constituents demonstrate with their witty wordplay that they are capable of deciding for themselves what should be celebrated. This is Shakespeare's nod to the class struggles that plagued ancient Rome as well as Elizabethan life. The tribunes' hypocrisy is comical—they simultaneously dismiss the plebians and grumble about clipping the feathers from "Caesar's wing" to bring him down to their level.

Caesar joins the crowd, and a soothsayer ominously warns Caesar to "beware the Ides of March." Caesar dismisses the soothsayer, and continues through the streets, amid the hearty cheering of the crowds. Cassius and Brutus, senators of the noble patrician class, discuss Caesar's popularity, and Cassius, seeing that Brutus appears to be troubled, begins his campaign to turn Brutus against Caesar. Although Brutus admits that he is out of sorts not because of Caesar but because of internal conflicts, Shakespeare gives us a hint that despite Brutus's unassailable reputation, he may be in such a state that Cassius's cozenage might gain traction.

Shakespeare signals that Brutus's convictions are malleable when Brutus responds: "The eye sees not itself but by reflection, by some other things." It is by this statement that we understand that Brutus, despite being described by the other characters as noble, honest, principled, and respected, is vulnerable. He admits that at this time, he can't know himself other than by seeing himself reflected in others.

Shakespeare offers us additional foreshadowing when Brutus asks Cassius, "Into what dangers would you lead me, Cassius, that you would have me seek into myself for that which is not in me?" It is revealed that Brutus loves Caesar, has no cause against him, and questions Cassius's motivations. Most who read or attend a performance of Julius Caesar already know the ending, so we are drawn into the narrative wondering how a character like Brutus, widely known to be full of integrity, could be taken down by the wily, "lean and hungry"–looking Cassius. We all know what's coming when Cassius poses the not-so-rhetorical question to fellow conspirator Casca: "For who so firm that cannot be seduced?"

112   **Shakespeare's Guide to Living the Good Life**

Cassius gives Brutus the hard sell, flattering him and recounting stories of Caesar's weaknesses, arguing that by comparison, Brutus is a far more deserving leader. According to Cassius, Caesar's physical infirmities, combined with an insatiable lust for power, render him exceptionally dangerous. In Cassius's initial conversation with Brutus, however, Caesar is offstage, repeatedly refusing the crown which the citizens are offering to their beloved conqueror and social reformer. Brutus's reticence signals to Cassius that stronger measures of persuasion are needed, so he asks one of his colleagues to write missives in different handwriting (as if from the commoners) extolling Brutus's virtues, expressing fears that Caesar will appoint himself king and disband the republic, and asking Brutus to take action to protect them.

In act 2, upon the ides of March, Caesar's wife, Calphurnia, has a premonition of Caesar's death by stabbing and pleads with him not to go to the senate that day. Similarly, Brutus's wife, Portia, realizes that he is not himself, and although he pretends to have a physical ailment, she knows that it is something else—a sickness of his own mind that disturbs him. She pleads with him to reveal his dark secret and relieve himself of distress, but he refuses, promising to tell her later. Unfortunately, two of his coconspirators knock on his door at that very moment, leading him away to gather for the attack, thwarting Portia's attempt to save her husband from himself.

Caesar, unlike Brutus, initially takes his wife's advice and agrees not to leave his home that day. Several of the coconspirators learn of this development, which will derail their plans, and they send

Decius to convince Caesar to reconsider. Decius tells Caesar that he will be laughed at if he reports to the senators that Caesar is afraid to leave his home, and when Caesar admits that he is heeding Calphurnia's warning Decius twists the premonition of Caesar being stabbed into a vision of the blood of Caesar spouting to all of Rome to revive its citizens, who will come to him requesting favors. Caesar is persuaded by Decius and agrees to participate in the ceremony at the senate.

Act 3 begins with Caesar and the senators walking from the street into the capitol, where Caesar is stabbed to death. The senators smear their hands and swords with Caesar's blood and move into the streets proclaiming their deed as representative of the death of tyranny. Mark Antony, who remained loyal to Caesar, requests an audience with Brutus to determine what happened. Brutus explains his reasons, but Mark Antony sees the fault in the conspirators' plan. He knows that Brutus will explain to the plebians, who are outraged, the reasoning behind the assassination, and he requests the opportunity to speak as well. Brutus, to his demise, agrees.

Brutus explains his reasons to the crowd, who are convinced by his words that the plot to kill Caesar was honorable until Mark Antony speaks, putting the plot into context, discrediting and humiliating Brutus with his persuasive rhetoric. Mark Antony repeatedly calls Brutus "an honorable man," but shows that he participated in a deed that was not honorable. After Mark Antony's speech, the crowd seeks revenge on the conspirators, who are driven from the city as Mark Antony mounts an army to defeat them.

Acts IV and V address the battles between the armies of Mark Antony, Brutus, and Cassius, and the play ends with both Cassius and Brutus "running on their swords" and killing themselves to avoid being taken by the armies of Mark Antony. One stupid mistake by Brutus leads to a series of consequences that ends in his death as well as that of most of the other assassins. In historical context, it also leads to the demise of the republic.

Julius Caesar is one of the most iconic of Shakespeare's tragedies, and this may be because there is much of our modern world in the personal and political motifs of this ancient story. The gullible Brutus, the oblivious Caesar, the crafty Cassius, and the opportunistic Mark Antony represent universal themes that play out in our homes, offices, places of worship, towns, and the world stage.

Many Shakespeare scholars believe that *Julius Caesar* was one of the first plays performed in the original Globe Theatre in 1599. The audience knew the story because of Thomas North's 1579 translation of Plutarch's *Lives of the Noble Grecians and Romans*, and many members of Shakespeare's audience had learned in grammar school that Caesar was an extraordinarily

Thinking for Yourself

skilled Roman general and politician whose military accomplishments included the invasion of Britain in 54 BCE. His success bred jealousy and fear among his peers, not only because he appeared to be consolidating power for himself, but because he had begun to institute populist reforms. Caesar's patrician detractors did not approve of Caesar conferring citizenship on those who had come under Roman rule through military defeat, establishing protections for marriage, constructing public libraries and marketplaces, granting legal relief to plebeians who were harmed by members of the elite, and conveying vast tracts of farmland to military veterans. These ancient Roman themes were particularly relevant during Elizabeth I's reign, where land use, political intrigue, and social climbing were part of Londoners' daily lives.

When I first read *Julius Caesar* as a freshman in college, I felt sorry for Brutus as an unwitting pawn in the conspirators' assassination plot against Caesar. *Julius Caesar* is often performed with an eye toward the machinations of ambition, power, politics, greed, and war. Although the play is certainly a commentary on politics from a macro level, I find the personal inner turmoil of Brutus and his failure to follow his own North Star to be Shakespeare's more compelling message, one that applies to all of us, whether we participate in politics or not. To live the good life, we have to think for ourselves.

Brutus, despite his well-documented nobility, honor, integrity, virtue, and respect for Caesar, is not immune to Cassius's

116   Shakespeare's Guide to Living the Good Life

blandishment. Brutus has a close friendship with Caesar, "loves him well," and "know[s] no personal cause to spurn at him." If the conspirators can turn Brutus to the dark side, their plan will succeed. "O, [Brutus] sits high in all the people's hearts, and that which would appear offense in us, his countenance, like richest alchemy, will change to virtue and worthiness." The villains realize all too well that their assassination will fail without the mark of decency that Brutus's reputation brings.

Cassius's strategy to win over Brutus is threefold: (1) stroke Brutus's ego through flattery; (2) paint a portrait of Caesar that renders him unfit to lead; and (3) appeal to Brutus's sense of civic duty by manufacturing citizens' handwritten requests for Brutus to unseat Caesar and save the republic. This triadic approach disables Brutus's ability to think for himself, which leads to the unfathomable—a cowardly act by a person of high integrity.

Brutus isn't the only one who fails to follow his internal guidance. Caesar ignores the warning signs that could save his life. A soothsayer tells him to "beware the Ides of March." His wife recounts a dream in which he is murdered and asks him not to attend the assembly on March 15. Thunder, lightning, and unusual storms engulf the city the night before his assassination. Rather than consider the import of these signs, Caesar falls prey to the same three-pronged assault on his ability to think for himself. When the conspirators realize that Caesar intends to forego the assembly at the capitol, they (1) stroke

Thinking for Yourself   117

his ego; (2) paint a portrait of the coward he will appear to be if he stays home out of fear; and (3) appeal to his duty to the citizens who attempted to crown him king the prior day. Caesar, like Brutus, cannot withstand the attack, and despite his better judgment is led by his executioners to the place of his slaughter.

Many of us know someone who has stood up for themselves and followed their own North Star when others pressured them against it. One of my favorite examples is Yvon Chouinard, an environmentalist and the founder of the outdoor retail company Patagonia. His commitment to the environment is so strong that, rather than sell the company or take it public when he reached the age of eighty (as conventional business doctrines would suggest), he and his family transferred their three-billion-dollar ownership in the company to a nonprofit collective, which will use the funds to combat climate change. Chouinard received no tax break for the donation that was made in 2022—rather, he paid over seventeen million dollars in taxes on the gift. Why did he do it? Because he believed that this was the best way to ensure that Patagonia's profits would be directed toward initiatives that would protect the planet and everyone who relies on it. Rather than use his power for his own financial gain, he employed it for the greater good.

This is an inspiring example of someone who chose to do what they believe is right, not for personal gain, but as a benefit to all. If we look, we can find other examples closer to home: a child who bucks the crowd to stand up to a bully; a parent who takes action to clean up their street as others complain that it's a hopeless cause; an employer who gives someone with no resume a chance to prove themselves. When we think for ourselves, we take action that is aligned with our values and we silence the naysayers. Shakespeare, through a tragic story that was well-known in the sixteenth century, shows us what happens when we choose not to follow our intuition and instead capitulate to the lies of those who want to maintain power for themselves.

Brutus and Julius Caesar initially craft lives built on integrity and their own moral compasses. Brutus was a revered member of the patrician class, lauded for his honesty and forthrightness. Caesar was a successful militarist and beloved populist reformer, his career defined by skillful decision-making. Both fall prey to the pressure of their peers, who use lies, cajolery, and a ticking clock to pressure them into following the conspiring crowd, to their mutual downfall.

In the case of Brutus, Shakespeare emphasizes the striking of the hours of the clock on the night that Brutus wrestles with the decision to betray his friend, and Cassius shows up at Brutus's house at 3:00 a.m. to make sure Brutus doesn't change his mind: "I have been up this hour, awake all night"; "Peace, count the clock"; "The clock has stricken three." Brutus, working on no sleep, is particularly vulnerable. His wife,

Thinking for Yourself

Portia, sees his distress and encourages him to confide his thoughts, but the conspirators arrive in the wee hours to make sure that Brutus is with them. The ticking clock, lack of sleep, early hour, and peer pressure all work against Brutus's ability to take the time to think for himself.

Caesar suffers the same fate. When he considers the warning of the soothsayer as well as his wife's dream of him bleeding to death and weighs the information presented to him, he decides to remain at home rather than attend the senate assembly. However, the conspirators cannot allow that to happen—they send Decius to Caesar's home, saying "I come to fetch you to the Senate House." Caesar replies, "Decius, go tell them Caesar will not come. . . . The cause is in my will. I will not come. That is enough to satisfy the Senate." Caesar is so close to saving himself here, but Decius spins Calphurnia's warnings into something positive, and then accuses Caesar of being a coward: "If Caesar hide himself, shall they not whisper 'Lo, Caesar is afraid?'" Caesar's fear of being called craven leads him to believe Decius's lies, and he abandons his own better judgment to follow the falsehoods, leading to his death.

Brutus and Caesar disregard their intuition, which ultimately leads to their undoing. Science says our intuition can be particularly helpful in detecting lies. Several published studies concur that when participants are asked to list pros and cons in determining whether someone is lying, their conclusions are

120   **Shakespeare's Guide to Living the Good Life**

less accurate than the participants who use their intuition to determine whether a statement is false.[1]

Shakespeare shows us the folly of disregarding our intuition and invites us to make a different choice. Following our inner guidance, thinking for ourselves, and standing in our own truths are ingredients that help us to live the good life. Staying strong in the face of pressure might feel scary, but with practice it becomes easier every day. With time, we can become the "masters of our fates."

Enactments

It can be challenging to listen to your intuition, especially when other people are offering conflicting messages. Use these enactments when you need to tune into the innate wisdom of your heart.

Buy Time to Decide

Sometimes the feeling of being pressured into a decision arises because the person pressuring you has created an artificial deadline. For example, when being pressured to decide on a big purchase, such as a car or home, we are often told that the offer expires at a certain time, that there are multiple offers, or that this is the last model on the lot. Although those circumstances may occasionally be true, they are often a ruse intended to force you to act immediately. Therefore, whenever you are faced with a big decision, consider whether you

Thinking for Yourself   121

can give yourself additional time to weigh your options. This reduces the influence of others and eliminates the obligation to give someone else what they are expecting.

If you're not sure how to buy yourself a little time, here are some examples of neutral responses that might assist when you're being pressured: "That timeline doesn't work for me." "I'll let you know when I can give you an answer." "Can I get back to you next week?" "This is an important decision and I don't want to rush it." Give yourself all the time and space you need to think for yourself.

Hone Your Intuition

Often the difference between hearing your inner voice (intuition) and repeating the statements of others (head-speak) is the feeling in your body. Intuition feels grounded and comforting, as if puzzle pieces are fitting into place. Head-speak feels like anxiety and restriction, as if you must do something to "prepare for the worst."

When faced with a challenge, a question, or a situation in which someone is pressuring or pushing you to make a decision, sit with the question and listen to what your inner voice sounds like as you contemplate the issue. Do the words feel like puzzle pieces fitting into place, or do they feel like a warning to stockpile something before it slips away? Does the voice sound like you, or does it sound like someone else? If it sounds like someone else, can you identify that person and determine where you've heard these words before? Really listening to the voice and how it sounds when you are considering a decision can give you clarity on whether you are hearing yourself or simply repeating something that you've been told over and over again. It is up to you to decide if those words resonate with you, or if they no longer serve you.

As these questions and challenges arise, keep a journal of your thoughts about them for clarity and focus on your value system and your need for action (or inaction). As you practice listening to your thoughts and identifying their origins, you may even use different colored pens and markers to distinguish them. I like to use purple for the inner voice that represents my intuition. As you learn and grow, your value system continues to develop, and a journal is a great way to chronicle your evolution.

Thinking for Yourself

Chapter Eight

Being of Service

Twelfth Night

The first line of *Twelfth Night* is, "If music be the food of love, play on." Orsino, Duke of Illyria, is in love with Lady Olivia, and we learn quickly that she is not interested in the duke's overtures. Lady Olivia is mourning the death of her brother, to whom she is so devoted that she has vowed to grieve in isolation for seven years.

Viola also knows the feeling of loss—she barely survived a shipwreck off the coast of Illyria, and she believes that her twin brother, Sebastian, is one of the casualties. She crawls to shore with the ship's captain, who relates Duke Orsino's sad story of unrequited love, which the captain knows because of his frequent travels to Illyria. Viola, in a foreign land without a penny to her name, decides to disguise herself as a eunuch, offering to serve Orsino as a musician, singer, and attendant. She changes her appearance, asks to be called Cesario, and begins her gender-bending journey with a new identity.

Meanwhile, best friends Toby and Andrew are planning a night of dancing and drinking. Sir Toby is the woeful Olivia's uncle, and he has tried to convince her that Sir Andrew is a good match for her, but Olivia wants nothing to do with men until her mourning period has ended. It doesn't matter to her that Andrew "plays o' th' viol-de-gamba, speaks three or four languages word for word without book, and hath all the good gifts of nature"; she has sworn off all suitors for seven years.

Viola (as Cesario) is taken into Orsino's service, and she immediately falls in love with him. He begs her to woo Lady Olivia in his name, and Viola reluctantly agrees. Viola woos Olivia on Orsino's behalf, and comically, Olivia falls in love with Viola. Olivia's philosophical jester, Feste, provides color commentary for the audience as Olivia chases after Viola, Viola pines for Orsino, and Orsino pesters Viola for news of Olivia's response. Throughout the mischief, Feste cracks jokes and comments drolly: "Foolery, sir, does walk about the orb like the sun, it shines everywhere."

Olivia's twin, Sebastian, is not lost at sea after all—he shows up in Illyria and befriends Antonio, who agrees to help him find his footing in this new land, giving him his money purse and instructing him to meet at the Elephant public house for food and lodging. Meanwhile, Toby convinces Andrew that he must challenge Viola to a duel, because Olivia has given Viola her ring while Andrew watched the encounter, and Toby surmises that this was done to make Andrew jealous. Toby encourages Andrew to show his love for Olivia by besting Viola in martial confrontation: "Why, then, build me thy fortunes upon the basis of valor. Challenge me the Count's youth to fight with him. Hurt him in eleven places. My niece shall take note of it, and assure thyself, there is no love-broker in the world can more prevail in man's commendation with woman than report of valor."

Viola and Andrew meet, but both are terrified to fight. Antonio happens upon them, and thinking that Viola is his new friend, Sebastian, Antonio draws his sword. Antonio is arrested and asks Viola for the money purse so he can pay his bond, but she doesn't understand. She gives him a bit of money for defending her, and Antonio feels confused and betrayed. As Antonio is taken away to prison, ranting and raving, he names his betrayer—Sebastian. Viola begins to hope that her brother is alive: "Prove true, imagination, O prove true, that I, dear brother, now be ta'en for you!"

We learn that Sebastian is so alive and well that when he meets Olivia in the town, she thinks he is Viola and drags him into the chapel to be married. Surprised and pleased with his good fortune, Sebastian happily agrees. Sometime later, Viola tells Orsino of Antonio's bravery and his strange request for a purse of money, and Olivia appears before them, newly wed and believing that Viola is the one with whom she recently exchanged nuptials. Duke Orsino is furious that the woman of his dreams foreswore her mourning for Orsino's eunuch, and Viola is perplexed, swearing that Olivia must be mistaken. Sir Andrew stumbles into the group calling for a surgeon, lamenting that Viola has presently beaten both him and Sir Toby with his sword, giving them both a "bloody coxcomb." Viola

Being of Service

is bewildered by this news as well, because she has not married or beaten anyone. Olivia instructs Feste to take Toby and Andrew to be treated, and at that very moment, Sebastian appears in the street.

Understanding dawns when Sebastian draws alongside his twin sister, apologizing for hurting his wife's kinsman, Sir Toby. Sebastian is thrilled to see his friend Antonio, who replies: "How have you made a division of yourself? An apple cleft in two is not more twin than these two creatures. Which is Sebastian?" Viola admits that she has been playing as a boy, and that her proclamations of love to Orsino have been the truth during her service to him:

And all those sayings will I overswear,
and all those swearings keep as true in soul
as doth that orbéd continent the fire
that severs day from night.
(*Twelfth Night*, act 5, scene 1)

Acknowledging that he has grown to love Viola, Orsino professes his love for her. The newly wed Olivia welcomes Orsino as a brother, Antonio recovers his money purse, Sir Toby marries Olivia's lady-in-waiting, Maria, and the twins, Viola and Sebastian, are blissfully reunited. Feste gives the informal epilogue, ending with this rhyming verse:

A great while ago the world begun,
with hey, ho, the wind and the rain,

but that's all one, our play is done,
and we'll strive to please you every day.
(*Twelfth Night*, act 5, scene 1)

Shakespeare knew that being of service takes us out of our comfort zones, and often creates lots of laughter in the process. *Twelfth Night*, with its theme of service to another, is one of the funniest of all of Shakespeare's comedies. The first recorded performance of *Twelfth Night* occurred at the Middle Temple Inn of Court on February 2, 1602, during the celebratory feast of Candlemas. This was part of the Christmas revels, much like *The Comedy of Errors* at the Gray's Inn of Court holiday celebrations several years prior. The performance of *Twelfth Night* was recorded by a barrister-in-training named John Manningham, who attended the play in Middle Temple Hall, a venue that today appears largely the same as it did during the original performance. Somehow this grand gallery managed to survive the Great Fire of London in 1666, the zeppelin raids of World War I, and the blitzkrieg of World War II. As a result, modern Shakespeare enthusiasts have been able to view his provocative performances in the same location where the Lord Chamberlain's Men first took the stage.

The themes of misrule, hijinks, pranking, relationships, and service are ones that would have resonated with the idealistic barrister trainees at Middle Temple. The drunken tomfoolery of Toby and Sir Andrew, the amiable yet sagacious tongue of Feste, and the earnest longing for love on the parts of Orsino, Viola, Olivia, and Sebastian would have fit perfectly with the rowdy Christmas festivities at Middle Temple. Winter was a time of celebration, but when the holiday decorations were dismantled, the optimistic young law students returned to their studies and their hopes to practice a trade in service to the public.

I recently saw a group of students in a troupe called the Bard Bus enact *Twelfth Night* in a small indoor theater in Saint Augustine. What struck me was the commitment and the acrobatic nature of the actors, made possible because of their youth and enthusiasm. They jumped, rolled, leaped, kicked, tumbled, and made full use of their bodies in this lighthearted play about mistaken identities, pranks, and being in love. These young students performed like I imagined the original Lord Chamberlain's Men troupe performed—with high energy and unfettered confidence, in service of the story. They were having the time of their lives and invited the audience to join them, which is exactly what I imagine the stage to have been like for Shakespeare and his mates. This was probably my favorite performance of *Twelfth Night*, and now I will always compare any other version to this marvelous rendition by the Bard Bus. It reminded me that Shakespeare was (and still is) for every member of society, not only for those who hold power or make the rules.

Shakespeare could have gone into politics (his father was an alderman), the family glove-making business, or some other more steady profession. Instead, he chose to share his creative talent and inspiration with the world. The choice to follow his passion is one that demonstrates the kind of service that is important—that which benefits the world and satisfies our own creative outlets. Be you an actor, musician, acrobat, writer, poet, publisher, visual artist, or simply someone who desires to put a smile on another's face, sharing your gifts with the world is the epitome of service and a simple hop, skip, and jump over to the good life.

Twelfth Night's alternate title, *What You Will*, may have been a nod to the theme of service in the play as well. In one scene, Olivia asks her steward, Malvolio, to give excuses for her when she doesn't want to see Duke Orsino. She offers Malvolio a few suggestions as to how to beg off for her, and then instructs him to come up with whatever else he can think of—"what you will"—such that she trusts him to use his own imagination in being of service to her. This is Shakespeare's more nuanced concept of service. It's not "do what I tell you" or "do what the group is doing," but rather the kind of service that permits you to explore your creative faculties to help out a friend, family member, or neighbor. It is evidence of Shakespeare's growing confidence in his art, adding more nuance to his plays,

Being of Service

experimenting with his new "fool," Robert Armin, who is known to have played Feste in *Twelfth Night*, and acknowledging that relationships are complicated and messy. With good intentions and combined effort, even the messiest of circumstances resolve themselves happily, if not creatively.

"Creative" is a great way to describe the characters in *Twelfth Night*, beginning with Viola. She decides that it will be easier to commend herself to the duke's service if she is dressed as a eunuch, and she does such a phenomenal job that Orsino begins to rely on her: "Cesario, thou know'st no less but all. I have unclasped to thee the book even of my secret soul." Viola is in love with Orsino, so the last thing she wants to do is convince Olivia to fall in love with him too. Nevertheless, Viola loves Orsino so much that she agrees to help: "I'll do my best to woo your lady," but says to herself in the next breath, "Yet a barful strife! Whoe'er I woo, myself would be his wife."

Toby's version of service is to keep his friend Andrew in town long enough to win Olivia's heart. Toby and Andrew spend their evenings dancing, drinking, laughing, singing, and enjoying the party life. Toby hopes that Andrew will marry his niece so that he can continue to carouse with his friend and keep the good times going. We're not sure that Andrew really wants to be in a relationship with Olivia, but Toby talks him into it, and he certainly enjoys Toby's company. Maybe that's why their more transactional and less altruistic service ends

132   **Shakespeare's Guide to Living the Good Life**

with the two of them in the hospital tending to their matching mohawk-shaped head wounds.

Antonio finds Sebastian washed up on the shore after the shipwreck and agrees to help him get on his feet in Illyria. This appears to be a true act of service; Antonio is known to have a bad reputation (at least according to Orsino), but when he meets Sebastian, he is ready and willing to redeem himself. Antonio explains his good deeds to the police when he is arrested:

> This youth that you see here
> I snatched one half out of the jaws of death,
> relieved him with such sanctity of love,
> and to his image, which methought did promise
> most venerable worth, did I devotion.
> (*Twelfth Night*, act 3, scene 4)

Antonio trusts Sebastian with his money purse, gives him the lay of the land, and doesn't hesitate to step in with his sword when Viola is threatened by Sir Toby and Sir Andrew. And in the end, his benevolent actions are rewarded.

Maria, Toby's long-suffering cousin and Olivia's lady-in-waiting, recognizes Toby's penchant for drinking and merrymaking, yet she puts up with his shenanigans because she knows he has a good heart. She goes so far as to help him play a prank on Olivia's pompous steward, Malvolio, and the pranksters have so much fun plotting and planning their roguery that Maria and Toby realize that they are meant for each other. Cousins marrying each other might be frowned upon today, but it was as common as a rainy day in Elizabethan England, and a fitting end for Toby and Maria.

When we think of service, many of us probably envision group activities, such as working at soup kitchens, rebuilding communities after natural disasters, volunteering at shelters, or donating to neighborhood food drives. Those types of service are wonderful; however, the kind of service that Shakespeare presents in *Twelfth Night* is more personal, and sometimes these smaller acts of service contribute to the good life as much as, if not more than, the big projects.

My twin daughters are the perfect example of this kind of service, and they've been showing me what it means to share their gifts in simple ways since the day they were born. They are natural caregivers and animal lovers, with two of the biggest hearts on the planet. One incident is etched in my memory with heartfelt tears: they were three years old and we were at a local shopping center. It was the end of the day, my hands were full of bags, and I couldn't hold both of their hands to take the escalator up to the level where our car was parked. One of the twins suddenly became terrified of the escalator. Mind you, she and her sister had ridden escalators many times, but for whatever reason this time it was different. We stood at the bottom of the escalator as I scanned the area for an elevator, because it seemed like the escalator was no longer an option. I could feel the panic rising in my daughter, even though I didn't understand it.

My other daughter looked at me, looked at her sister, held out her chubby little fingers, and said, "Don't be scared. I'll help you. Hold my hand." Seeing the encouragement in her sister's eyes, my frightened twin tentatively took her sister's outstretched palm in her own, and they stepped onto the moving stairs together. They were both so proud of themselves that they rode the other escalator back down, just to ride this one up again, giggling with pure delight. Writing this paragraph, envisioning that day, and remembering the look of jubilation on those angelic round faces is part of living the good life. I'm grateful that my little darlings blessed me with that experience.

That's how pure and simple an act of service can be. Seeing that someone needs help, knowing that you have the ability and desire to assist, and taking action can completely transform another person's life. No act of service is too small. My toddler went from terrified to triumphant in less than a minute, all because her sister saw a need, knew that she could help, and acted. My daughters have been doing that for each other since before they could walk, and it reminds me that these kinds of small gestures can have enormous impacts on others. Helping someone lift their bag into the overhead compartment on an airplane, offering to watch someone's pet if they are going to be away from home, lending the use of a pickup truck to help a neighbor move, or volunteering to accompany someone to

Being of Service

an appointment if they're nervous relieves the person receiving the assistance, makes the one in service feel needed, and enriches the lives of everyone who witnesses it.

These small acts of service enhance our time on this planet, confirm that we are loved and valued, and give meaning to our lives. Studies have shown that volunteering in any form offers significant health benefits to the volunteer, including lower rates of depression and anxiety, higher rates of self-esteem and satisfaction, and in some instances creates a community or support system with aligned interests.[1] The health benefits of service are so well documented that some physicians prescribe nonmedical, social volunteering activities to patients as part of personalized plans for health improvement.[2] Prescriptions may include volunteering at a museum or library, helping to run events that the patient is interested in, such as holiday celebrations or fundraising walks, or working one-on-one as a tutor or mentor.

But while the benefits of volunteering through established programs or nonprofits are well supported, being generous with your time and your talents need not be a formal thing. A British study published in 2021 concluded that well-being increased with higher numbers of service-related activities, but there was no difference between formal, structured volunteering and informal, unstructured volunteering.[3] In fact, one study found that *less* formal types of service (offering to take out your neighbor's trash, for example) may be more altruistic in nature, and therefore provide better positive effects and higher self-esteem.[4]

Shakespeare makes it clear in *Twelfth Night* that the easiest way to serve is to use the gifts we have to benefit others. The best example of this is Shakespeare's sagacious fool, Feste, who has been gifted with many talents (songwriting, dancing, a beautiful singing voice, and a brilliant mind) and uses them all to delight the audience and aid the other characters. For example, when he's trying to lift Olivia's spirits at the beginning of the play, he offers us his wisdom about the notion of the afterlife:

FOOL
Good madonna, why mourn'st thou?

OLIVIA
Good Fool, for my brother's death.

FOOL
I think his soul is in hell, madonna.

OLIVIA
I know his soul is in heaven, Fool.

FOOL
The more fool, madonna, to mourn for your
brother's soul, being in heaven.
(*Twelfth Night*, act I, scene 5)

Being of Service   137

Touché, Feste, touché. I had to sit with that little exchange for a few minutes the first time I read it. He uses his wit to console Olivia while simultaneously advising her that her extensive period of mourning is unwarranted. Being so witty, talented, and fun-loving, Feste gets away with many of these bold statements made to characters of a higher station, and they love him for it. Sir Andrew goes so far as to praise him as follows: "I had rather than forty shillings I had such a leg [for dancing] and so sweet a breath to sing, as the Fool has." Everyone who comes in contact with Feste leaves the encounter entertained, enlightened, and energized. As in many Shakespeare plays, the Fool is the smartest character on stage and the one most clearly in service of the message.

Feste also upholds the notion that service is something that we enjoy: when he employs his singing and dancing talents to entertain Orsino, the latter tries to pay him for "his pains" and Feste responds, "No pains, sir. I take pleasure in singing, sir." Shakespeare invites us to do the same, to serve others by using our innate talents.

Enactments

Volunteering increases feelings of positivity, reduces stress, and has been shown to release the good-feeling hormone, dopamine. It provides a sense of meaning and appreciation for the volunteer and the recipient. It also doesn't require a schedule or an invitation—random acts of kindness are a simple and impactful way to offer service to loved ones as well as strangers. The best part is that often, when you offer a random act of kindness to someone, it makes them so happy that they pay it forward, creating a domino effect of gratitude and appreciation.

Offer a Random Act of Kindness

Here are seven of my favorite random acts of kindness. Feel free to try a different one each day and write in your journal about the feedback you get from others, the way you felt, and how the act of kindness affected your day.

1. Pay for the person behind you in the drive-through. (This is a popular one, and the smile you put on the person's face behind you is a joy that lasts all day.)

2. Write a note of encouragement or an uplifting statement (something as simple as "you are special and loved") and place it in the front of a popular library book for someone to find.

3. Post on the social media page of someone you follow, telling them how much you appreciate the messages they share.

4. Send a heartfelt email to a friend, coworker, or family member, pointing out your favorite things about them and showing how you value your relationship with them. (If you want to channel Shakespeare for

Being of Service

this one, grab your quill and ink and write them an actual letter on paper.)

5. Go through your home and find a few household items that you no longer use. Bag or box them up and take them to a donation center of your choice, or leave them out with a "free" sign on them—maybe you'll meet a neighbor and make a new friend.

6. Bring your neighbor's trash cans in for them after they've been emptied. You'll put a curious smile on your neighbor's face as they wonder about their anonymous benefactor.

7. Make or buy a favorite food for a friend, coworker, family member, or neighbor. If they like a special kind of tea, or have a preferred candy, leave it on their doorstep when they least expect it.

Volunteer to Be Someone's Wingmate

Two of the characters in *Twelfth Night* acted as a wingmate— Viola for Orsino and Sir Toby for Sir Andrew. You can be someone's wingmate, too. If you know someone who isn't enjoying the dating process, invite them to a gathering of singles and facilitate the mingling. If you know someone who really wants to go somewhere, like to the movies, a concert, a play, or a sporting event, but they don't want to go by themselves, offer to accompany them. Better yet, surprise them with the tickets. This also applies if they want to take a class (dance,

140   **Shakespeare's Guide to Living the Good Life**

pottery, cooking, foreign language) but can't find anyone to share the experience—volunteer to participate. It's a wonderful gift for someone, a way to spend time with a friend or family member, and you might enjoy the experience as much as they do. These small moments are what living the good life is all about.

Chapter Nine

Friendship

The Winter's Tale

The play opens with childhood best friends Leontes (King of Sicilia) and Polixenes (King of Bohemia) discussing Leontes's request to have his friend extend his holiday in Leontes's kingdom. Polixenes begs off because he has his own kingdom to attend to and he worries that he's already stayed away too long. Their conversation is jovial and lighthearted, and the love between these lifelong friends is obvious. Despite Leontes's best efforts, he can't convince Polixenes to stay, so Leontes enlists his very pregnant wife, Hermione, to help him make the case. She successfully does the job, and Leontes praises her convincing words, saying that she "never spok'st to better purpose." They are happy, healthy, and in love. Hermione and Polixenes walk away to continue their discussion about his extended stay as Leontes plays with his young son, Mamillius.

Suddenly and shockingly, Leontes sees Hermione and Polixenes in conversation and is overcome with jealousy. Leontes's paranoid brain imagines that they are cavorting romantically under his nose, and the audience hears Leontes talk himself into a fabricated nightmare. In a "tremor cordis," Leontes convinces himself not only that Hermione is sleeping with Polixenes, but that she is carrying his child. (Yes, Shakespeare boldly drops the heavy irony that if Hermione had not done what her husband asked in persuading his best friend to stay, he would have never conceived the idea that Hermione was unfaithful.)

In a bizarre rage, Leontes imprisons Hermione, claims the child in her belly is not his, and directs one of his trusted courtiers, Camillo, to poison Polixenes. Camillo, faced with the lose-lose situation of killing an innocent man or disobeying an order of the king, decides to "forsake the court" and help Polixenes escape back to Bohemia. Hermione, while in her jail cell, gives birth to Leontes's daughter, Perdita. Hermione's attendant, Paulina, brings the baby to Leontes to persuade him that he is the father. Paulina points out the baby's features that match Leontes's own, but he refuses to listen. Leontes instructs Paulina's husband, Antigonus, to transport the baby to a far-off land, and Antigonus hastens away with the newborn, dropping her on the "desert" shores of Bohemia.

Meanwhile, Leontes's friends and courtiers try to convince him of Hermione's innocence. Though he does not change his mind, he agrees to send two Sicilian lords, Cleomenes and Dion, to the Oracle of Delphi for a divine proclamation on the issue of his wife and the newborn child. As is the custom, the priests of Apollo's divine oracle will write the truth on a scroll and seal it, to be transported

144   **Shakespeare's Guide to Living the Good Life**

back and opened only in front of King Leontes. This ensures that the message is truly from the oracle, Pythia.

While Cleomenes and Dion are away, Hermione is put on trial, and she gives an impassioned speech proclaiming her innocence. The irrational Leontes is unmoved. Cleomenes and Dion return, break the seals of the scroll, and reveal the message:

Hermione is chaste, Polixenes blameless,

Camillo a true subject, Leontes a jealous tyrant,

his innocent babe truly begotten; and the King shall

live without an heir if that which is lost be not found.

(*The Winter's Tale*, act 3, scene 2)

Leontes immediately reacts in anger, yelling, "There is no truth at all i' th' oracle." Leontes, in disparaging Apollo, draws the wrath of the gods. A servant appears to report that Mamillius dropped dead at the very moment Leontes spoke. Hearing that her son is gone, Hermione falls and Paulina notes, "This news is mortal to the Queen. Look down and see what death is doing." Hermione is whisked away by Paulina and the attendants, and Leontes realizes that he has invited the wrath of the gods, lamenting, "Apollo's angry, and the heavens themselves do strike at my injustice." The loss of his son, wife, and daughter finally convinces Leontes of his grave error, and he admits, "I have too much believed mine own suspicion." His epiphany is too little, too late.

Friendship

Sixteen years later, Perdita is a Bohemian shepherdess, having been raised by a simple Bohemian shepherd and his son, Autolycus. Camillo has become Polixenes's trusted courtier in that same land. Polixenes's son, Florizell, falls in love with Perdita, and they plan to marry, against Polixenes's wishes. The king opposes the union because he believes Perdita to be a simple shepherdess, unworthy of his son's affection. Camillo helps the lovers escape to Sicilia, and instructs them to present themselves to King Leontes as Prince and Princess-to-Be, come to bring greetings from Polixenes. They follow Camillo's plan and the haggard and penitent King Leontes welcomes them. His life has been an unending series of miseries ever since his fear-based insanity took control of his senses.

Leontes learns from Perdita's adopted father (who has also traveled to Sicilia), that Perdita is Leontes's long-lost daughter. Polixenes and Camillo arrive in Sicilia, and as Leontes begs forgiveness, the two kings are reunited. Polixenes is relieved to know that his son's betrothed is Princess Perdita, the young infant thought lost so many years before. The final surprise for Leontes is a gift from Paulina to the king, a statue of Hermione. As Leontes gazes upon it, the statue comes to life and Hermione embraces her husband and daughter. The king is forgiven by all and family and friends are reunited.

This play is an example of friendship that withstands extreme circumstances, and I've always wondered whether its poignancy is attributable to Shakespeare's own deep friendships with his fellow actors and creative collaborators. Most scholars believe that *The Winter's Tale* was one of Shakespeare's later plays, written in late 1610 or early 1611. The first recorded performance was at the Globe on May 15, 1611, and that same year it was performed for King James I at Whitehall Palace. The play appears to be based on a popular story by Robert Greene that was published in 1588 called *Pandosto: The Triumph of Time*, but that story ended in tragedy, with Leontes's suicide. Shakespeare, possibly fatigued after writing a string of tragedies such as *Macbeth*, *Coriolanus*, and *Antony and Cleopatra*, made his version into a comedy, continuing to delve into the theme of amnesty through the passage of time. He also added the characters Paulina, Antigonus, and Autolycus, which developed one of the core motifs of *The Winter's Tale*: friendship.

It is believed that the actor Richard Burbage, son of Shakespeare's theatrical mentor James Burbage, was Shakespeare's best friend. Richard Burbage played some of Shakespeare's most iconic characters, such as Hamlet, Othello, and Macbeth, and many academic researchers postulate that Shakespeare wrote Hamlet specifically for Richard. James Burbage died shortly before *Hamlet* was penned, and his death was likely a shocking loss for his son, Richard, and his protégé, Will. Other actors in the Lord Chamberlain's Men (later the King's Men),

Friendship 147

such as John Heminges and Henry Condell, were also close friends of Shakespeare, and thanks to them, we have the first folio of Shakespeare's works, published in 1623. The theme of friendship is not only evident in the play itself, but in the lives of the creative artists and actors who brought it to the stage.

Unlike Shakespeare's other plays, my first encounter with *The Winter's Tale* was *not* love at first sight. I read it during my sophomore year of college, and it infuriated me. What could I learn from a horrifying four-hundred-year-old story of a privileged husband's sudden descent into jealousy, which wreaks havoc on his family, ruins his life, kills his wife and son, banishes his infant daughter, and exiles his best friend? In *Julius Caesar*, Brutus suffered from failing to listen to his inner knowing. In *The Winter's Tale*, Leontes suffered from an equally devastating failure: believing his paranoid ego's fear-based hallucinations. These seemingly opposite examples are why Shakespeare is one of the greatest writers to chronicle the complexities of the human condition.

As a student of literature, I knew Shakespeare was considered a master of tragedy, but the injustice and unexplained delirium in *The Winter's Tale* offended my collegiate sensibilities. I could find no reasonable explanation for Leontes's devolution: there was no history of paranoia, no greed, no evidence that Hermione was unfaithful, no backstory about the best friends being frenemies—it was simply Leontes's worried mind convincing him that his worst fear was real. But it wasn't.

148   **Shakespeare's Guide to Living the Good Life**

At least Hamlet could blame his insanity on the loss of his father. But here, Leontes had everything he ever wanted, and he literally threw it away because of a dread-filled delusion. *The Winter's Tale* irritated me immensely, and I promptly tossed it in the pile of literary pablum at the end of the semester. Happily, it was the play's theme of friendship that brought me back to a new appreciation of *The Winter's Tale* after my own gap of time. A friend was reading a contemporary version of *The Winter's Tale* and reintroduced me to the original. This time around, I found it much more satisfying and enlightening than I could have imagined, having gained a perspective that was not available when I was younger. Friends do those things for each other, which is why friendship is such an important part of living the good life.

The play begins with best friends, Leontes and Polixenes, sharing childhood memories together in a lovely setting following a holiday with their families in Leontes's kingdom, Polixenes recalling:

We were as twinned lambs that did frisk i' th' sun

and bleat the other at th' other. What we changed

was innocence for innocence. We knew not

the doctrine of ill-doing, nor dreamed

that any did. . . .

(*The Winter's Tale*, act 1, scene 2)

Friendship   149

Unfortunately, their close bond is soon broken, and through the catastrophically stupid actions of Leontes we are introduced to the different degrees of friendship through the relationships between other characters.

When Hermione is falsely accused of all manner of betrayal and misdeeds, it is her lady-in-waiting, Paulina, who shows us what friends do for each other in extreme circumstances. After Hermione gives birth to Perdita and Leontes disavows the newborn as his child, Paulina risks her position and possibly her life to convince Leontes that the baby is his, hoping that the sight of his child will cure his madness:

If she dares trust me with her little babe,
I'll show 't the King and undertake to be
her advocate to th' loud'st. We do not know
how he may soften at the sight o' th' child.
(*The Winter's Tale*, act 2, scene 2)

King Leontes is not swayed, and Paulina barely escapes with her life, but she continues to protect, defend, and support her friend, Hermione, ultimately bringing her back to life, thus offering salvation to Leontes.

Camillo's actions in amity also aid in Leontes's salvation, a concept that was an integral part of the Elizabethan worldview. Leontes directs Camillo to poison Polixenes, but Camillo knows immediately that Leontes is misguided. It takes a great

150   **Shakespeare's Guide to Living the Good Life**

deal of courage to stand up to one's friends (not to mention employers), and yet Camillo shows his bravery when he makes the decision to defy Leontes's instructions. Camillo knows that he is putting his relationship with Leontes (and his life) at risk by going against Leontes's wishes, but he also knows that if he kills Polixenes, he would be murdering an innocent man. Like Camillo, our best friends and closest colleagues are mirrors for us, sometimes showing us our flaws even when we want to look away.

Polixenes's relationship with Leontes represents another version of friendship, one in which the companions have known each other so long that they don't judge each other when they falter. Granted, Leontes's faltering is of an extreme variety, but Shakespeare lets us know throughout the play that aside from that one moment of insanity that leads Leontes down a nightmarish path, he has otherwise been a true friend to Polixenes and a good person. Polixenes could have held a grudge, vowing never to have anything to do with Leontes again, but Shakespeare chose to show us an example of reconciliation between the friends. Leontes is penitent and ashamed, and his remorse appears genuine. Under those circumstances, it seems generous and somehow fitting that Polixenes agrees to revive their friendship. Maintaining the relationship and forgiving his friend are more important than the appearance of weakness that he might demonstrate by reconciling with

Friendship   151

Leontes. Polixenes and the other extraordinary friends in *The Winter's Tale* serve as examples for us all.

My partner and I have been together for a long time, and we were friends for years before we were married. In fact, our wedding song was "You're My Best Friend" by Queen. We have held space for each other through many difficult situations, and when I think of what Paulina did for Hermione, standing up to the insanely angry Leontes, defending Hermione's honor and integrity, and supporting Hermione through the pain of childbirth, it reminds me of the many times my partner has stood up for me, defended me, and supported me in my hard times. He is the first person to take my side in any dispute and is a cheerleader who never lets me forget how much he loves me.

When I would have a difficult or stressful day with an especially maddening or aggressive opposing counsel, I could come home and vent to my partner, who immediately jumped to my defense: "That's outrageous! I can't believe you have to put up with that. Who are they? What's their number? What's their address? I'll show them they can't treat you like that!" I recognize that he didn't really intend to confront whoever caused my bad day, but knowing that he empathized with me, had my back, and was willing to defend me and do anything in his power to make things right, meant the world to me.

Science helps explain the reasons why this is so. A 2016 study tested participants to determine whether receiving support (defined as the experience that one is loved and cared for by others, esteemed and valued, and part of a social network of mutual assistance and obligation) led to positive neurobiological outcomes. The results revealed that receiving support benefits health and well-being, showing improvement in the neural pathways that are associated with better health outcomes. The study also showed that receivers of support were less vulnerable to stress.[1]

Similarly, a 2020 study reported in the *Journal of Humanistic Psychology* found that there are significant psychological benefits to receiving real-life altruism, the kind of support friends give to one another. The results show that 75 percent of the participants who had received an unexpected altruistic offering confirmed that the experience strongly changed their optimism about human nature, trust in social relationships, appreciation for life, sense of gratitude, self-esteem, sense of being valued by others, empathy for others, motivation to help others, energy and enthusiasm in general, and religious faith.[2]

Another study showed that receiving support from coworkers in ways that were not part of the coworkers' job descriptions (i.e., altruistic) increased positive outcomes at work and reduced work-family conflict. In this study, altruism is defined as behavior that benefits another, while being apparently detrimental to the one performing the behavior.[3] The actions of Hermione in *The Winter's Tale* would fit this definition of altruism because it is arguably detrimental for her to trust her husband again after what occurred. Hermione, like many of Shakespeare's heroines, however, seems to know something that is difficult for us to understand: grace, mercy, compassion, and forgiveness are qualities that lead to happy outcomes for both the giver and the receiver.

Have you ever surprised a friend or coworker by responding to an offense with generosity or altruism? We, like Leontes, are so accustomed to being punished for our sins that when a friend offers us empathy, grace, or altruism, we sometimes don't know how to respond. Leontes was prepared to suffer for the rest of his life because of the horrible things he had done to his wife and son:

> One grave shall be for both. Upon them shall
> the causes of their death appear, unto
> our shame perpetual. Once a day I'll visit
> the chapel where they lie, and tears shed there
> shall be my recreation. So long as nature
> will bear up with this exercise, so long
> I daily vow to use it. Come, and lead me
> to these sorrows.
> (*The Winter's Tale*, act 3, scene 2)

Instead, Paulina, Hermione, Polixenes, Camillo, and Perdita showed him that their friendships, their connections, and their love were more important than anything he could have

154   **Shakespeare's Guide to Living the Good Life**

done to hurt them. This is Shakespeare's example to us of a path to the good life. It may be difficult, but the rewards are far beyond our imagination.

Enactments

Most of us have never made an error of judgment as serious as Leontes does in *The Winter's Tale*, but we have all needed a friend's grace and compassion at some time in our lives. Use the following enactments to reflect on your friendships and the lasting impact they've had on you.

Make a Palace of Friendship Blueprint

One of the first places that *The Winter's Tale* was performed was at Whitehall Palace, the enormous Tudor residence of the English monarchs from Henry VIII to William and Mary. In light of this play about the importance of friendship, I invite you to create a blueprint for your own palace, one that is created by and through the friendships you've had in your life.

Think of the types of friendships you've had in your life, such as long-term friendships (a childhood neighbor with whom you've remained close, a high school buddy, or a college roommate), friendships for a specific time in your life (preschool moms or dads group, 5k training partner), friendships from shared experiences (military colleagues, work friends), friendships with different furry companions or pets over the years, and any other allies you can think of. Each of

Friendship   **155**

these friends (or groups of friends) will represent a room in your friendship palace. Think of it as a creative layout of your favorite relationships.

Grab some paper and colored pencils or pens. Design and sketch your friendship palace. Give it as many rooms and features as your imagination leads you to add. Remember, this is only for you, so don't judge your drawing skills or worry that anyone else is going to see it. Have fun with it!

Every blueprint has notes to accompany the drawing, so off to the side of the drawing, write what you love and value about this special friend or group of friends. For example, it could be things like "doesn't judge me for my choices," "has watched me laugh so hard I spurted milk from my nose,""cried with me when my beloved dog passed," "learned to ride a bike with me," or "eats pizza with me every Sunday night." Let your imagination carry you through a remembrance and appreciation of these friendships.

If you feel called, connect with the people you have identified. Tell them what they mean to you, and invite them to make their own friendship palace blueprints.

Mission to Mars

We have many friends that carry us through some of the darkest times in our lives, but as we move on, change, and evolve, sometimes we lose touch with those friends. Other times, we lose those friends to what Shakespeare calls "the gap of time."

156   Shakespeare's Guide to Living the Good Life

This enactment reminds us to appreciate what makes these friendships special.

Think about a friend that you've lost (either by death, losing touch, or a falling out). Imagine what you would say to them if you could meet with or talk to them again. One way to start the conversation in your mind is to imagine that they were chosen for a mission to Mars, which means that they would leave and possibly not come back. Imagine that you would not be able to see them face-to-face for a long time, if ever. Write a letter to them, telling them what their friendship meant to you, how you feel about losing touch with them, what effect they've had on your life and the choices you've made, and the nature of your hopes and dreams for them. When you're finished, meditate on whether it feels right to dispose of the letter (by burning or shredding, for example), or if it would be helpful to retain it and look back on it from time to time. Are there any epiphanies or realizations that shed light on your current friendships? Do the contents of the letter inspire you to reach out to your close friends? The gap of time holds mysteries and miracles for us all if we take the time to pay attention to our friendships and close relationships.

Friendship

Chapter Ten

Forgiveness

The Tempest

The Tempest begins with a great storm at sea in which the sky "pour[s] down pitch" and the wild waves rise to mount the sky. Alonso, the King of Naples; his son Ferdinand; Alonso's brother, Sebastian; Antonio, the Duke of Milan; Alonso's counselor, Gonzalo; and a crew of sailors are fighting for their lives on a ship being tossed about on the ocean. The ship cannot withstand the tempest and they are all thrown into the sea.

Miranda, daughter of Antonio's estranged brother, Prospero, observes the sinking ship and laments to her father the tragedy of the lost souls. In response, Prospero assures her that the sailors are fine; the tempest is his doing. He confesses to Miranda that twelve years prior, he was the Duke of Milan, and she a beloved three-year-old princess. Preoccupied with his library of esoteric books, Prospero didn't notice his traitorous brother plotting against him. Antonio conspired with the King of Naples to oust Prospero from his position, grabbing Prospero and Miranda in the middle of the night and putting father and daughter out to sea in a "rotten carcass of a butt" with no sail, tackle, or mast. Prospero and Miranda somehow survived (partly because of provisions stashed for them by the "noble Neapolitan, Gonzalo") and when they landed on this magical island, Prospero studied the books Gonzalo had stowed on the boat.

It is this magical study in isolation that enabled Prospero to become a great sorcerer. When Antonio and Alonso sail close to the island, Prospero understands that he must act to raise the tempest:

> By accident most strange, bountiful Fortune,
>
> now my dear lady, hath mine enemies
>
> brought to this shore; and by my prescience
>
> I find my zenith doth depend upon
>
> a most auspicious star, whose influence
>
> if now I court not, but omit, my fortunes
>
> will ever after droop.
>
> (*The Tempest*, act 1, scene 2)

Prospero summons Ariel, a nature spirit previously imprisoned in a tree by a witch named Sycorax. Prospero extricates Ariel from the tree with his magic, and Ariel thereafter does Prospero's bidding:

> I come
>
> to answer thy best pleasure. Be't to fly

to swim, to dive into the fire, to ride

on the curled clouds,

to thy strong bidding task,

Ariel and all his quality.

(*The Tempest*, act 1, scene 2)

Ariel confirms that those on Antonio's ship have been saved. Ariel enchants the ship's crew with a sleeping spell, allowing their aristocratic passengers to swim to land. Alonso's son Ferdinand is separated from the others, and Ariel brings him to a place near Prospero's cave. Sycorax's son, Caliban a "poisonous slave, got by the devil himself," overhears Prospero's conversation with Ariel, and when Ariel is dismissed, Caliban confronts Prospero, cursing him: "A southwest blow on you and blister you all o'er." Prospero and Caliban had previously been on friendly terms, teaching each other their respective forms of magic and witchcraft while Miranda served as Caliban's reading tutor. However, the relationship quickly soured when Prospero caught Caliban attempting to rape Miranda. Caliban and Prospero have been feuding ever since, Prospero now keeping Caliban under control with his magic.

On the other side of the island, Sebastian and Antonio attempt to murder King Alonso in his sleep, but Ariel deters them by waking Alonso and Gonzalo in time to see the conspirators with their swords drawn. Sebastian and Antonio make hollow excuses, yet Gonzalo does not believe them. Ariel performs additional feats of magic, creating a banquet feast for the hungry castaways that

Forgiveness   161

abruptly disappears when they attempt to eat. As time passes, Ariel's magical tricks stir the consciences of the conspirators, and Gonzalo observes that they are beginning to mend their ways.

On yet another part of the island, Alonso's butler, Stephano, and Alonso's jester, Trinculo, encounter Caliban fetching wood. The three are soon drunk after downing Stephano's bottle of wine. Caliban, emboldened by Stephano's kindness and his drunkenness, decides to escape Prospero's rule and take up with his new friends, saying "Freedom, high-day! High-day, freedom? Freedom, high-day, freedom!" Caliban convinces Stephano and Trinculo to attack Prospero, burn his books, and take Miranda as their reward.

Miranda encounters the handsome, young Ferdinand, and the two quickly fall in love. Prospero invites Iris (goddess of the rainbow), Ceres (goddess of agriculture), and Juno (queen of the gods and protector of marriage) to perform a masque celebrating Miranda and Ferdinand's engagement. The goddesses sing and dance a blessing for the couple's union, a beautiful scene that is cut short when Prospero realizes that Caliban and "his confederates" are at that moment plotting to take his life.

The plot is foiled by Stephano and Trinculo themselves, who are distracted by Prospero's wizarding laundry hanging on a line. Full of wine and shenanigans, they don Prospero's robes and pretend they are kings of the island. They're having so much fun that they completely forget that they are supposed to be killing Prospero. Everyone meets outside Prospero's cave, and the grand magician greets Alonso, Antonio, Sebastian, and Gonzalo with great

162   **Shakespeare's Guide to Living the Good Life**

theatrics. He announces that he is the rightful Duke of Milan and he intends to reclaim his position. Alonso is reunited with Ferdinand, who reveals that he is engaged to Prospero's daughter. Alonso agrees to return Prospero to his rightful title as Duke of Milan, and Prospero forgives Antonio for his betrayal. Ariel restores the castaways' ship and awakens the crew from their magical slumber, and Prospero agrees to tell the story of his life on the island as they make preparations to return to Milan. Prospero's last act on the island is to release Ariel, saying "Then to the elements be free, and fare thou well."

Shakespeare understood that forgiveness is a far more influential expression of emotions than revenge. Forgiveness, like magic, has the capacity to transform. Some have described the performances of Shakespeare's plays as magic, combining raw emotion, existential musings, slapstick comedy, and captivating wordplay. *The Tempest* offers all of this and more, which is why it has been a perennial favorite. As one of the last four plays that Shakespeare wrote before his death in 1616, *The Tempest* shows the bard's growth as both a philosopher and a playwright. Whereas other plays such as *Love's Labour's Lost* and *The Two Gentlemen of Verona* provide more lighthearted entertainment with lots of laughs, *The Tempest* is a mature and enduring artistic creation that contemplates the emotional panoply of the human experience. Shakespeare expertly weaves elements of fantastical magic and mystical nature into a narrative that explores the weighty themes of control, power, betrayal, imprisonment, and freedom.

Prospero's complexity is an example of Shakespeare's talent for creating a character who is simultaneously human and archetypal mage (a class that includes Merlin, Gandalf, and Dumbledore, to name a few). Like these other wizard archetypes, Prospero is old and wise, perhaps given to forgiveness because he's lived it all— the good, the bad, and everything in between.

Some academics believe that Shakespeare injected some of himself into Prospero, their evidence being that *The Tempest* was one of the last plays that Shakespeare wrote alone before his death, and that it includes his retirement speech, which makes reference to all the places his thespian troupe had performed ("cloud-capped towers, the gorgeous palaces, the solemn temples, the great globe itself"), and passes the mantle to the next generation as Prospero blesses the youngsters Miranda and Ferdinand, concluding that "we are such stuff as dreams are made on, and our little life is rounded with a sleep." Prospero's speech at the wedding of Miranda and Ferdinand is highly sentimental; knowing that it was written as Shakespeare's life drew to a close is a revelation that must have shocked and delighted the audience. For me, Prospero's speech carries the same emotional charge as when Toto pulls back

164   Shakespeare's Guide to Living the Good Life

the green curtain to reveal the true mastermind behind the great and powerful Oz. One of the reasons Shakespeare's art endures is because he put so much of his heart into his works, embodying the wizard archetype in the realm of literature, and demonstrating that in order to express ourselves authentically, we have to be vulnerable.

The foremost example of forgiveness in *The Tempest* is Prospero's exculpation of his traitorous brother, Antonio, and Antonio's coconspirator, the King of Naples. It is easy to view Prospero as the wronged victim who takes the high road and decides to forgive an egregious act of betrayal. Shakespeare, however, is never one to make his characters two-dimensional. Prospero the magician is a far more complex character with actions of his own that beg for forgiveness, particularly through his relationship with the nature spirit, Ariel, whose indentured servitude appears to be lasting longer than expected. We learn through dialogue that Prospero rescued Ariel from imprisonment in a tree prior to the events in *The Tempest*. In exchange, however, Prospero requires Ariel to do his bidding for a period of time, beginning with the invocation of the great squall. Prospero relies on Ariel and selfishly extends his indenture despite Ariel's good works and requests for freedom. Prospero raises the tempest, but he cannot perform the act alone. It is Ariel who darkens the sky, brings the deafening thunder, creates the mist from sea and air, enhances the lightning with blazing fires aboard the king's ship, nestles the ship in a nook where it will

Forgiveness 165

be hidden and protected, and puts the mariners to sleep safe under the hatches.

It is also Ariel who spurs Prospero to empathy, which leads to him forgiving his betrayers, noting that if Prospero could see the traitors bemoaning their predicaments, his "affections would become tender." After giving it some thought, Prospero agrees:

> Though with their high wrongs I am struck to th' quick
> yet with my nobler reason 'gainst my fury
> do I take part. The rarer action is
> in virtue than in vengeance. They being penitent,
> the sole drift of my purpose doth extend
> not a frown further. Go, release them, Ariel.
> (*The Tempest*, act 5, scene 1)

The significance of Prospero's forgiveness of the traitors cannot be overstated. His home, title, and friends have been taken from him, and his daughter, who should have been raised as a cosseted princess, is alone with him on an island with only a witch-damned monster for company. This forgiveness is mirrored by Ariel, who has reason to hold a grudge against Prospero but instead carries out his spirit responsibilities admirably, even spurring Prospero to forgive when he has been wronged.

One of the most painful experiences of my teenage life occurred when I was set up on a blind date. A friend (let's call her Mara) was dating a boy from another school; he had asked her to the dance and wanted her to find a date for his friend. We met at Mara's house and the four of us drove together. But soon after arriving, my date ghosted me. Being from a different high school, I didn't know anyone else at the dance, and I spent most of the night hiding in the bathroom wondering what had happened to my date. Mara, who had a penchant for bluntness, came into the bathroom and I asked her where he had gone. She said, "I don't really know how to say this, so I'm going to say it plainly—he said you're too ugly to be seen with, and he's getting a ride home with someone else."

I spent the next two hours sobbing in the bathroom. Days and weeks later, my emotions moved from sadness and shame to anger. Who could be so cruel? Why would a person say something so heartless? What had I done to deserve that treatment? I'd like to say that forgiveness came to me during those teenage years, but in truth, I hadn't yet been introduced to Shakespeare's Prospero, and I didn't understand the power of forgiveness.

After reading the play, and seeing what forgiveness offers to the forgiver, I realized that holding on to my anger was hurting *me*. My well-being was more important to me than obsessing over a heartless and superficial high school boy. His family owned a farm and ran a stall at the local farmers market, so I envisioned myself walking up to the stall one day many years later, whereupon seeing me he would fall to his knees and beg

Forgiveness 167

me to forgive him for being such a contemptuous idiot. After playing that fantasy in my head a few times, the tragedy at the dance eased its grip on me, and I was able to forgive the lunkhead. Garnering peace through forgiveness isn't quick or easy, but it's a huge part of living the good life.

A 2016 study found that forgiveness is associated with lower stress for the person who forgives, which leads to better mental health.[1] This applies to both self-forgiveness and forgiveness of others. Researchers have concluded that forgiveness interventions can be effective for lessening levels of perceived stress, anger, and negative feelings induced by hurtful interpersonal transgressions.[2]

In 2020, the National Institutes of Health published a study that found that forgiveness correlated with substantially reduced symptoms of depression, anxiety, hopelessness, and loneliness.[3] In reviewing this data, it is important to note that there are two kinds of forgiveness that have been studied: decisional forgiveness and emotional forgiveness. As you might guess, decisional forgiveness is making a commitment to forgive, which includes the manner in which you might treat the individual who has wronged you (including yourself). The far more difficult goal is to achieve emotional forgiveness, a state in which the negative emotional charge that you feel toward the person who has caused you harm has dissipated, such that you feel the forgiveness in your body.

168   Shakespeare's Guide to Living the Good Life

Many of the studies analyze the effects of certain forgiveness protocols. One such protocol was the topic of a conference held at Harvard University in April 2023, entitled "Forgiveness: Interdisciplinary Perspectives." A team of international researchers presented mini-studies of the effect of the REACH protocol on individuals who had experienced the effects of war in places such as Ukraine, South Africa, Colombia, Hong Kong, and Indonesia. The number of participants in this international trial was more than in all previous studies on forgiveness combined.[4] The results show that forgiveness plays an important role in global public health, and the popularity of this study is such that the methodology is freely available for anyone to download and apply at home.

The REACH protocol for forgiveness is as follows:

R: Recall the hurt. Face that you have been hurt, but make a decision to forgive and not pursue retaliation.

E: Empathize with the person who hurt you. Work to understand why you may have been wronged, allowing you to heal from hurt and give forgiveness.

A: Altruistic gift. Forgive unselfishly.

C: Commit. Write a note to yourself about who you forgave to help the forgiveness last.

H: Hold on to your forgiveness. If the feelings of resentment or the mental replay of the event arise, remember that you have offered forgiveness, and hold on to that decision.

The professor who developed the program experienced a personal tragedy that makes his work on the topic of forgiveness all the more compelling. In the early hours of New Year's Day, 1996, Everett Worthington's mother was brutally murdered in her home. Worthington recalled that he saw a baseball bat in the corner of a room the day they discovered his mother's body, and he vowed to beat the murderer's brains out with it.

Worthington had been a marriage counselor for fourteen years prior to his mother's murder, and had recently submitted a manuscript for a book entitled "To Forgive Is Human." In many interviews he has given over the years, he emphasizes that the model of forgiveness he developed does not replace or shorten any periods of grief, and it does not require an abandonment of justice. He also admits that it is difficult work that takes significant effort. It took him a long time to forgive his mother's killer, who was not brought to justice due to mishandling of evidence and a botched confession. By dint of hard work, he was able to apply his own REACH protocol to his family's circumstances, and the forgiveness he extended

170   **Shakespeare's Guide to Living the Good Life**

brought him peace that he could not find elsewhere. All of this shows that we have the power to reclaim our peace of mind.

Prospero both offers and seeks forgiveness in *The Tempest*, showing that we as humans are often on both sides of the equation. He admits his ill treatment of Ferdinand, whom he disparaged upon learning that Miranda had fallen in love with him. Prospero finally comes around and asks Ferdinand for pardon:"If I have too austerely punished you, your compensation makes amends, for I have given you here a third of mine own life." Ferdinand, flush with love for Miranda, immediately forgives Prospero, saying "As I hope for quiet days, fair issue, and long life, with such love as 'tis now, the murkiest den, the most opportune place, the strong'st suggestion our worser genius can shall never melt." The joy of forgiveness is felt by the forgivers and the forgivees who, like us, are often one and the same, depending on the circumstances.

Enactments

Whether you feel as if you've done something in need of absolution or you've been holding on to a long-remembered offense against you, the following enactments will help you tap into the transformative power of forgiveness.

Write the Apology You Want to Hear

Think about a person who hurt you and whom you can't seem to forgive. Write an apology as if it were coming from that person, and include everything that you wish the person would say to you to change your perspective on the situation. Imagine what circumstances may have led them to hurt you, or struggles and challenges that caused them to turn their wounds on you. Read the apology out loud, or have a friend or partner read it out loud to you. What emotions do you feel? Did writing and/or hearing the apology soften your hurt and anger? Take out the apology and review it periodically until you notice a willingness to offer forgiveness.

Another variation of this is to role-play a conversation between you and the wrongdoer. Put two chairs facing each other, and sitting in the first chair, let loose on the imaginary wrongdoer, telling them exactly how you feel, as if you are reading out criminal charges in a courtroom. Then switch chairs and respond as you imagine the perpetrator would respond. Continue switching chairs and extending the conversation until you have fully expressed all of your feelings. This is what acting is all about! When you're finished, notice how you are feeling and write it in a journal.

Find a Forgiveness Role Model

Consider a person you admire who has offered forgiveness in difficult circumstances. People across the globe have suffered atrocities, and a rare few have managed to forgive their offenders. Some examples are Nelson Mandela, Eva Mozes Kor, and Immaculée Ilibagiza. Feel free to find a role model of forgiveness that resonates with you and reflect on the reasons they give for forgiveness. Meditate on those reasons, and write down those that feel aligned to you. Do you notice any tension leaving your body? Does this help you to move into a space of forgiveness?

Become the Archetypal Magician

To do this meditation, find a quiet place where you can sit or lie down comfortably and remain undisturbed for twenty minutes. Once comfortable, close your eyes and imagine yourself as the ancient wizard archetype, such as Prospero, Merlin, Gandalf, Galadriel, Dumbledore, or Yoda. If it helps you to get into character, envision your enchanted appearance (regal robe or whimsical fairy wings?), magician's lair (castle, cave, or cottage?), and surrounding sounds (lapping waves or whistling winds?). Get creative as you embody your favorite maven. Invoke the qualities that your archetype displays, such as wisdom, tolerance, patience, perceptiveness, understanding, thoughtfulness, and forgiveness. Invite those qualities into your body and let them inhabit your being. Now imagine yourself in a situation where you will express those qualities, bringing them to fruition. Do you feel different? Are you standing taller? This archetype is an elder who has seen everything, knows what they want, and are willing to share it with others. What kind of elder do you want to be? How will you use your wisdom and knowledge to benefit the world?

Forgiveness

Epilogue: You Are Divine
Sonnet 18

Many Shakespeare performances end with an epilogue: a few lines in which one or more of the actors directly addresses the audience to share conclusory remarks about the play, sometimes offering a blessing to the attendees, or, continuing the comedy, begging forgiveness if the actors somehow offended the crowd. In true Shakespearean form, this book's epilogue is meant for you, the reader, to take the words of my favorite Shakespearean sonnet as a blessing to carry with you after you've finished this book.

The journey through the themes of hospitality, imagination, compassion, persistence, communication, exploring nature, thinking for yourself, being of service, friendship, and forgiveness brings us to a place that Shakespeare inhabited and continues to invite us to dwell in: the good life. Shakespeare's stories address the core of our human existence, a core that is as poignant, stirring, and meaningful today as it was when Shakespeare dipped his quill into ink and scratched it onto a piece of parchment four hundred years ago. These themes are not distant or esoteric; they are the foundation of our relationships with each other, nature, the world, and our inner truth. As such, we can tap into them at any time.

I hope that the enactments in this book help you connect to your version of the good life, whether it looks like the boisterous enthusiasm of the asshead weaver Nick Bottom, the quiet compassion of the wise heiress Portia, or the wacky and heartfelt hospitality of the Antipholus and Dromio twins. Whether your life is already good or you are struggling to find a bit of good during difficult times, these enactments are intended to bring a sense of fun and meaning to your life.

I encourage you to read the following sonnet, imagining that the Bard of Avon, Will Shakespeare, is in the room with you, watching you read what he has written just for you. Never forget that you are splendid, marvelous, powerful, and divine. That's your guide to living the good life.

Shall I compare thee to a summer's day?

Thou art more lovely and more temperate.

Rough winds do shake the darling buds of May,

And summer's lease hath all too short a date.

Sometime too hot the eye of heaven shines,

And often is his gold complexion dimmed;

And every fair from fair sometime declines,

By chance, or nature's changing course, untrimmed;

But thy eternal summer shall not fade,

Nor lose possession of that fair thou ow'st,

Nor shall death brag thou wand'r'est in his shade,

When in eternal lines to Time thou grow'st.

So long as men can breathe, or eyes can see,

So long lives this, and this gives life to thee.

(Sonnet 18)

Epilogue: You Are Divine

Acknowledgments

To business that we love we
rise betimes and go to 't with delight.

You said it, Will! Writing this book has been a childhood dream come true, one that manifested in an extraordinary way. Dougall Fraser invited me to attend a Celebrate Your Life event in 2022 where Hierophant Publishing offered a contest for attendees: submit a book proposal, and if your proposal is chosen, Hierophant will publish your book. I submitted what I thought was a crazy idea about sharing Shakespeare's wit and emotional wisdom with the world, and I'm so glad I did, because that book is now in your hands!

To Randy, thank you for your razor-sharp insights, delivered with kindness and humor. To Hilary, thank you for your generosity and exceptional brainstorming skills. To Grace, thank you for your love of Shakespeare and your unshakable support for me and this project. Special thanks to the folks at Celebrate Your Life, who provided a life-changing experience that resulted in a meaningful collaboration with the team at Hierophant. And finally, thank you to my husband, Dave, whose creativity, humor, and unconditional love inspire me to follow my passions every day.

Notes

Chapter One: Hospitality

1. Dana Sparks, "Mayo Mindfulness: The Health Benefit of Laughter," Mayo Clinic News Network, July 11, 2018, https://newsnetwork.mayoclinic.org/discussion/mayo-mindfulness-the-health-benefit-of-laughter/.

2. Jonathan P. Rogers, Edward Chesney, Dominic Oliver, Thomas A. Pollak, Philip McGuire, Paolo Fusar-Poli, et al., "Psychiatric and Neuropsychiatric Presentations Associated with Severe Coronavirus Infections: A Systematic Review and Meta-analysis with Comparison to the COVID-19 Pandemic," *The Lancet Psychiatry* 7, no. 7 (2020): 611–627, https://doi.org/10.1016%2FS2215-0366(20)30203-0.

3. "Covid-19 Pandemic Triggers 25% Increase in Prevalence of Anxiety and Depression Worldwide," World Health Organization, March 2, 2022, https://www.who.int/news/item/02-03-2022-covid-19-pandemic-triggers-25-increase-in-prevalence-of-anxiety-and-depression-worldwide.

4. Roger O'Sullivan, Annette Burns, Gerard Leavey, Iracema Leroi, Vanessa Burholt, James Lubben, et al., "Impact of the COVID-19 Pandemic on Loneliness and Social Isolation: A Multi-Country Study," *International Journal of Environmental Research and Public Health* 18, no. 19 (September 23, 2021): 9982, https://doi.org/10.3390/ijerph18199982.

5. Nicholas Leigh-Hunt, David Bagguley, Kristin Bash, Victoria Turner, Stephen Turnbull, Nicole Valtorta, et al., "An Overview of Systematic Reviews on the Public Health Consequences of Social Isolation and Loneliness," *Public Health* 152 (2017): 157–171, https://doi.org/10.1016/j.puhe.2017.07.035.

6. "Social Isolation and Loneliness Increase the Risk of Death from Heart Attack, Stroke," American Heart Association, August 4, 2022, https://newsroom.heart.org/news/social-isolation-and-loneliness-increase-the-risk-of-death-from-heart-attack-stroke.

7. R. I. M. Dunbar, "Breaking Bread: The Functions of Social Eating," *Adaptive Human Behavior and Physiology* 3, no. 3 (2017): 198–211, https://doi.org/10.1007/s40750-017-0061-4.

Chapter Two: Imagination

1. Jeffrey M. Ellenbogen, Peter T. Hu, Jessica D. Payne, Debra Titone, and Matthew P. Walker, "Human Relational Memory Requires Time and Sleep," *Proceedings of the National Academy of Sciences* 104, no. 18 (May 2007): 7723–7728, https://doi.org/10.1073/pnas.0700094104.

2. Erin J. Wamsley, Matthew Tucker, Jessica D. Payne, Joseph A. Benavides, and Robert Stickgold, "Dreaming of a Learning Task Is Associated with Enhanced Sleep-Dependent Memory Consolidation," *Current Biology* 20, no. 9 (May 2010): 850–855, https://doi.org/10.1016/j.cub.2010.03.027.

3. Alejandra Rosales-Lagarde, Jorge L. Armony, Yolanda del Rio-Portilla, David Trejo-Martine, Ruben Conde, and Maria Corsi-Cabrera, "Enhanced Emotional Reactivity after Selective REM Sleep Deprivation in Humans: An fMRI Study," *Frontiers in Behavioral Neuroscience* 6, no. 25 (June 2012), https://doi.org/10.3389%2Ffnbeh.2012.00025.

Chapter Three: Compassion

1. Archontia Mantelou and Eirini Karakasidou, "The Effectiveness of a Brief Self-Compassion Intervention Program on Self-Compassion, Positive and Negative Affect and Life Satisfaction," *Psychology* 8, no. 4 (March 2017), https://doi.org/10.4236/psych.2017.84038.

2. Olga M. Klimecki, Susanne Leiberg, Matthieu Ricard, and Tania Singer, "Differential Pattern of Functional Brain Plasticity after Compassion and Empathy Training," *Social Cognitive and Affective Neuroscience* 9, no. 6 (June 2014): 873–879, https://doi.org/10.1093/scan/nst060.

3. Tania Singer and Olga M. Klimecki, "Empathy and Compassion," *Current Biology* 24, no. 18 (September 2014), https://doi.org/10.1016/j.cub.2014.06.054.

Chapter Five: Communication

1. Baldesar Castiglione, *The Book of the Courtier* (1528; Project Gutenberg, 2022), translated by Leonard Eckstein Opdycke, https://www.gutenberg.org/files/67799/67799-h/67799-h.htm.

2. Michael H. Kernis and Brian M. Goldman, "A Multicomponent Conceptualization of Authenticity: Theory and Research," *Advances in Experimental Social Psychology* 38 (2006): 283–357, https://doi.org/10.1016/S0065-2601(06)38006-9.

3. Elisa De Stefani and Doriana De Marco, "Language, Gesture, and Emotional Communication: An Embodied View of Social Interaction," *Frontiers in Psychology* 10 (September 2019), https://doi.org/10.3389/fpsyg.2019.02063.

Chapter Six: Communing with Nature

1. Yuanchao Gong, Yang Li, Linxiu Zhang, Tien Ming Lee, and Yan sun, "Threats of COVID-19 Arouse Public Awareness of Climate

Change Risks," *iScience* 25, no. 11 (November 2022), https://doi
.org/10.1016/j.isci.2022.105350.

2. "Great Expectations: Making Hybrid Work *Work*," Microsoft Work
Trend Index Annual Report, March 16, 2022, https://www.microsoft
.com/en-us/worklab/work-trend-index/great-expectations-making
-hybrid-work-work.

3. Marcia P. Jiminez, Nicole V. DeVille, Elise G. Elliott, Jessica E. Schiff,
Grete E. Wilt, Jaime E. Hart, et al., "Associations Between Nature
Exposure and Health: A Review of the Evidence," *International Journal
of Environmental Research and Public Health* 18, no. 9 (May 2021): 4790,
https://doi.org/10.3390%2Fijerph18094790.

4. Stephen Kaplan, "The Restorative Benefits of Nature: Toward an
Integrative Framework," *Journal of Environmental Psychology* 15, no. 3
(September 1995): 169–182, https://doi.org/10.1016/0272
-4944(95)90001-2.

5. Roger S. Ulrich, Robert F. Simons, Barbara D. Losito, Evelyn
Fiorito, Mark Miles, and Michael Zelson, "Stress Recovery During
Exposure to Natural and Urban Environments," *Journal of Environmental Psychology* 11, no. 3 (September 1991): 201–230, http://dx.doi.
org/10.1016/S0272-4944(05)80184-7.

Chapter Seven: Thinking for Yourself

1. Justin S. Albrechtsen, Christian A. Meissner, and Kyle J. Susa, "Can
Intuition Improve Deception Detection Performance?" *Journal of
Experimental Social Psychology* 5, no. 4 (July 2009): 1052–1055, https://
doi.org/10.1016/j.jesp.2009.05.017.

Chapter Eight: Being of Service

1. Eric S. Kim, Ashley V. Whillans, Matthew T. Lee, Ying Chen, and Tyler J. VanderWheele, "Volunteering and Subsequence Health and Well-Being in Older Adults: An Outcome-wide Longitudinal Approach," *American Journal of Preventative Medicine* 59, no. 2 (August 2020): 176–186, https://doi.org/10.1016/j.amepre.2020.03.004.

2. Amadea Turk, Stephanie Tierney, Geoff Wong, Joy Todd, Helen J. Chatterjee, and Kamal R. Mahtani, "Self-Growth, Wellbeing and Volunteering—Implications for Social Prescribing: A Qualitative Study," *SSM—Qualitative Research in Health* 2 (December 2022), https://doi.org/10.1016/j.ssmqr.2022.100061.

3. Katey Matthews and James Nazroo, "The Impact of Volunteering and Its Characteristics on Well-Being after State Pension Age: Longitudinal Evidence from the English Longitudinal Study of Ageing," *The Journal of Gerontology* 76, no. 3 (March 2021): 632–641, https://doi.org/10.1093/geronb/gbaa146.

4. Jerf W. K. Yeung, Zhuoni Zhang, and Tae Yeun Kim, "Volunteering and Health Benefits in General Adults: Cumulative Effects and Forms," *BMC Public Health* 18, no. 1 (July 2017): 736, https://doi.org/10.1186/s12889-017-4561-8.

Chapter Nine: Friendship

1. Tristen K. Inagaki, Kate E. Bryne Haltom, Shosuke Suzuki, Ivana Jevtic, Erica Hornstein, Julienne E. Bower, and Naomi I. Eisenberger, "The Neurobiology of Giving Versus Receiving Support: The Role of Stress-Related and Social Reward-Related Neural Activity," *Psychosomatic Medicine* 78, no. 4 (May 2016), https://doi.org/10.1097/PSY.0000000000000302.

2. Edward Hoffman, Jenniffer Gonzalez-Mujica, Catalina Acosta-Orozco, and William C. Compton, "The Psychological Benefits of

Notes   185

Receiving Real-Life Altruism," *Journal of Humanistic Psychology* 60, no. 2 (February 2017), https://doi.org/10.1177/0022167817690280.

3. Sajid Haider, Carmen De-Pablos-Heredero, and Monica De-Pablos-Heredero, "The Paradox of Citizenship Cost: Examining a Longitudinal Indirect Effect of Altruistic Citizenship Behavior on Work-Family Conflict Through Coworker Support," Frontiers in Psychology 12 (2021), https://doi.org/10.3389/fpsyg.2021.661715.

Chapter Ten: Forgiveness

1. Loren L. Toussaint, Grant S. Shields, and George M. Slavich, "Forgiveness, Stress, and Health: A 5-Week Dynamic Parallel Process Study," *Annals of Behavioral Medicine* 50, no. 5 (October 2016): 727–735, https://doi.org/10.1007/s12160-016-9796-6.

2. George M. Slavich, Grant S. Shields, Bailey D. Deal, Amy Gregory, and Lauren L. Toussaint, "Alleviating Social Pain: A Double-Blind, Randomized, Placebo-Controlled Trial of Forgiveness and Acetaminophen," *Annals of Behavioral Medicine* 53, no. 12 (December 2019): 1045–1054, https://doi.org/10.1093/abm/kaz015.

3. Katelyn N. G. Long, Everett L. Worthington Jr., Tyler J. Vander-Weele, and Ying Chen, "Forgiveness of Others and Subsequent Health and Well-Being in Mid-Life: A Longitudinal Study on Female Nurses," *BMC Psychology* 8 (October 2020), https://doi.org/10.1186%2Fs40359-020-00470-w.

4. "Largest-Ever Study on Forgiveness Shows Decreased Anxiety and Depression," Templeton World Charity Foundation, April 20, 2023, https://www.templetonworldcharity.org/blog/REACH-forgiveness-study.

About the Author

Kim Bradley is an author, lawyer, blogger, and Shakespeare enthusiast who has immersed herself in the heart-based wisdom of the Bard of Avon for more than four decades. She graduated with dual degrees in English and political science from Duke University, where she studied the plays of William Shakespeare and their effects on American literature and modern life. She lives in northeast Florida, exempt from public haunt, on a bank where the wild thyme blows. Connect with her at www.kim-bradley.com.

San Antonio, TX
www.hierophantpublishing.com